D1014034

Best Easy Day Hikes
Hawaii: Kauai

Help Us Keep This Guide Up to Date

Every effort has been made by the author and editors to make this guide as accurate and useful as possible. However, many things can change after a guide is published—trails are rerouted, regulations change, facilities come under new management, etc.

We would appreciate hearing from you concerning your experiences with this guide and how you feel it could be improved and kept up to date. While we may not be able to respond to all comments and suggestions, we'll take them to heart and we'll also make certain to share them with the author. Please send your comments and suggestions to the following address:

Globe Pequot Press
Reader Response/Editorial Department
P.O. Box 480
Guilford, CT 06437

Or you may e-mail us at:

editorial@GlobePequot.com

Thanks for your input, and happy trails!

Best Easy Day Hikes Series

Best Easy Day Hikes
Hawaii: Kauai

Suzanne Swedo

FALCONGUIDES

GUILFORD, CONNECTICUT
HELENA, MONTANA

AN IMPRINT OF GLOBE PEQUOT PRESS

For John B.

FALCONGUIDES®

Project editor: Julie Marsh
Layout artist: Kevin Mak
Maps: Design Maps Inc. © Morris Book Publishing LLC

Library of Congress Cataloging-in-Publication Data is available on file.
ISBN 978-0-7627-4350-6

Printed in the United States of America

10 9 8 7 6 5 4 3 2 1

Contents

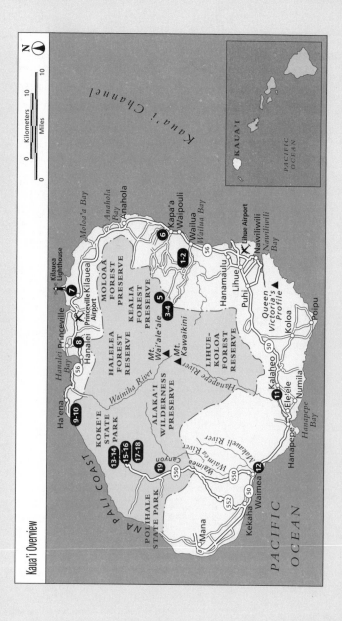

Kaua'i Overview

Acknowledgments

Thanks to everyone who shared their knowledge and enthusiasm for outdoor Kaua'i, including Paulette Burtner at Koke'e Museum, who knows everything there is to know about local trails; Nancy Merrill from Limahuli Garden and Preserve; and Jim DiMora, who loves Kauai's birds. For help and company on the trail and for assistance and support of every kind imaginable, thanks to Jo and Dave Acree, Melinda Goodwater, Chris Haun, Pat Medley, and Meryl Leventhal.

Kaua'i, the Garden Island

Kaua'i, the Garden Island, is a hiker's island. It is small but less densely populated and less developed than its larger neighbors, and it has lots of trails for everybody from kids to mountaineers, at least one of them world famous. The Kalalau Trail along the Na Pali Coast is one most hikers want to tick off their life lists, along with trekking in Nepal or summiting Half Dome. There are beach strolls, explorations of deep valleys dripping with mist, hikes to pools fed by waterfalls or to viewpoints over some of the world's most beautiful canyons and shorelines. You can even wander through a swamp among tropical flowers and birds found only on this island.

The island is not undeveloped because of any lack of scenic beauty or charm, but because the very things that make it so lush and green—the torrential rainfall in the mountains and the dramatic cliffs plunging straight down to the sea—make road building and other development expensive and impractical. Tourists cluster in Poipu on the southern coast where a short section of beach is crammed with hotels and condos and traffic, but these are confined to a relatively small stretch of the shore. Lihue, the civic center and home of the airport, bustles with local business during the week but is not primarily a tourist town. Hanalei on the north shore has retained its charm because there simply isn't anywhere for it to spread, though the posh resort of Princeville is not too far away.

Kaua'i is the oldest of the four major Hawaiian Islands, though at five to six million years it's still a baby in geologic terms. Its longer exposure to wind and rain has allowed its bare lava to break down into soil so that more green things can grow. Those green things are nourished by the 450 inches of rain per year that trade winds bring to Mount Wai'ale'ale near the center of the island, making it the wettest place on earth. Beneath Mount Wai'ale'ale lies the Alaka'i Swamp, where layer upon layer of lava created by the single gigantic volcano that built Kaua'i is so dense that water does not drain away but collects in permanent pools. That same dense, impermeable lava erodes away so slowly that Kaua'i is higher in elevation than O'ahu, even though the latter is younger. Outdoor lovers will be pleased to know that the high country in the center of the island is too cool for mosquitoes to thrive, even where there is standing water. Kaua'i has lost fewer of its native bird species to the introduced mosquito-borne diseases that have been largely responsible for decimating bird populations on other islands.

The windward cliffs of the Na Pali Coast have been eroded into sharp ridges and valleys where rainwater is funneled back into the sea, but some of the rock layers are so hard that the stream channels extend only partway down from the crest, forming hanging valleys over which innumerable waterfalls pour. All of this—tropical sun, rainfall, extreme topography, resistant rock, and relatively less human interference—makes Kaua'i the richest by far of all the Hawaiian islands in spectacular plant and bird species that live nowhere else in the world.

All this also makes for lots of exciting exploration for foot travelers. Be prepared for a few challenges though—most of them related to *mud*. Kauai's famous red dirt (used as dye for the "genuine Red Dirt T-shirts" for sale on all the islands) turns to slimy clay when wet, and it is wet more often than not. Wear expendable clothing and hike with caution. Hiking poles are especially handy on Kaua'i.

Maps

The *Kaua'i Recreational Trail Map* (1:50,000), with the eastern half of the island shown on one side, the western on the other, is published by *Na Ala Hele,* the state Trails and Access System, and is available from the Hawai'i Division of Forestry and Wildlife in Lihue. You can get it in person for a fee at the DOFAW office, 3060 Eiwa Street, Room 306 in Lihue, or by mail for a slightly larger fee (money order or cashier's check only) from the same address (the zip code is 96766). The *Northwestern Kaua'i Recreation Map* by Earthwalk Press (1:31,400) is waterproof and a little sturdier, more detailed, and easier to read, but more expensive. The USGS 7.5-minute topographic maps are helpful but frequently out of date. Kaua'i has experienced so much flooding, exacerbated by steep cliffs and soil denuded by goats, that trails frequently have to be rebuilt and rerouted, and the USGS can't keep up. The museum at Koke'e State Park has detailed maps of the trails in that area that include information about natural and cultural history.

The shaded relief map of *Kaua'i* published by the University of Hawai'i Press, available in bookstores and elsewhere. is the best for exploring the island as a whole. It gives you a bird's-eye view of the geography of the island with its mountains, waterfalls, beaches, and of course, its roads and highways.

Getting Around

As on all of the Hawaiian Islands, if you do not live here, you will have to rent a car to access most trails. It is easy to do in Lihue at the airport, but in summer and on weekends, a reservation is a must. Many of the trails around Koke'e State Park that would qualify as easy are only accessible by four-wheel-drive roads, and even these are impassible after heavy rain. You can rent an SUV, but the tires are bound to be inadequate, and you're likely to get stuck or slide down a slippery hill anyway, and car rental companies won't rescue you. Fortunately these roads are beautiful, great for hiking, and have very little traffic, so many are incorporated into day hiking routes.

Accommodations

Lihue has a couple of inexpensive hostels, but there isn't much other cheap lodging on Kaua'i with the major exception of the housekeeping cabins at Koke'e State Park. Call (808) 335-6061 or visit www.thelodgeatkokee.net for more information. There is also a campground nearby. The Hawai'i Department of Parks and Recreation has several other campgrounds on the island, for which you will need a permit. You can sometimes get a permit from a park ranger at the site, or you can pick one up in person from the Kaua'i Department of Public Works, 4444 Rice Street, Room 150 in Lihue, or send for an application by mail (the zip code is 96766). The phone number is (808) 241-6670. Permits for camping at state parks are available from the Hawai'i Department of Land and Natural Resources, Division of State Parks, 3060 Eiwa Street, Room 306, Lihue 96766; (808) 274-3444.

A Few Words of Caution

Most of Kauai's trails are on lava that has weathered to red clay that becomes as slippery as butter on glass when it gets wet. Hikes that are easy in dry weather may become much more difficult when it has been raining long and hard, and narrow footpaths clinging to mountainsides can become downright dangerous. Hiking poles and good shoes are recommended.

Weather Patterns

Weather on Kaua'i is usually lovely, with temperatures between 70 and 80 degrees year-round at sea level and cooler temperatures in the high country. There are essentially two seasons: Summer (May through October) is only slightly warmer than winter, and the trade winds blowing from the northeast usually keep even the warmest days pleasant, so hiking is good all year. The big difference between the seasons is in the amount of precipitation. Rainfall is lighter and of shorter duration in summer; in winter it is more frequent, heavier, and lasts longer.

All but the steepest and sloppiest trails are fun and safe year-round unless there is a Kona storm. These occur when for some reason or other the trade winds fail and rain from the southwest (instead of the northeast) pours down buckets for days on end.

Make sure some of your hiking clothes are synthetic rather than cotton. Synthetic clothing is fast drying and wicks moisture away from your skin. It can be surprisingly chilly at 4,000 feet around Koke'e State Park, where many of the best trails originate. A Windbreaker and rain gear are essential items to carry in your day pack. Make sure you have a brimmed hat and lots of sunscreen, too. The sun is directly overhead this close to the equator.

Drinking Water

All free-flowing water on Kaua'i must be treated before drinking. Here, leptospirosis is the most significant water-borne disease-causing organism. Spread primarily by rats and mice, it is a bacterium that can cause flulike symptoms including fever, diarrhea, nausea, muscle pain, chills, headache, and weakness, and if not treated with antibiotics can lead to very serious problems like heart or kidney failure.

Chemical treatment or boiling will take care of drinking water, but you can get leptospirosis by swimming in contaminated water as well as by drinking it. You are advised not to swim in fresh water if you have a cut or broken skin, and not to put your head underwater. That said, swimming and splashing in Hawaii's streams and pools is one of the most popular pastimes in the islands, and nobody appears to be overly concerned. But you should be aware that there is a risk.

Stream Crossings

Speaking of water, it rains a lot on Kaua'i and there are several hikes in this guide that involve stream crossings. Some are shallow enough to rock-hop, though rocks are usually rounded and slick and wading is safer. If it has been raining long and hard, streams may be too high and fast to ford safely.

Unexpected flash floods are especially dangerous and have killed lots of people, especially along the Na Pali Coast. Many of Hawaii's streams flow down almost perpendicular cliffs, and floods may originate high up in the rainy mountains while you are strolling unaware along the coast under sunny skies. If a stream appears muddy, or if you can hear rocks rolling along the streambed, turn around! Tropical vegetation often releases tannins into the water, making it be dark in color and hard to see through even under ordinary conditions, but swirling mud is serious.

Waves, Currents, and Riptides

The seas around the islands have weird patterns. There are lovely quiet coves perfect for snorkeling, and big regular waves for surfing, but in some places riptides can pull you off your feet and sweep you out to sea in an instant.

Never turn your back to the ocean when exploring tide pools or walking along sea cliffs. A rogue wave can sneak up on you any time. Beaches where it is not safe to swim are almost always clearly marked with warning signs, and the signs mean business!

Hawai'i has experienced tsunamis or tidal waves at rare intervals in its history, which have killed many. You will probably notice yellow civil defense warning sirens on posts along most windward coastlines. If these begin to blow, get to higher ground immediately.

Losing the Trail

Established trails are usually easy to follow. If there is any ambiguity, the clearest, most defined trail is usually the right one. Sometimes trails become so badly eroded by people going their separate ways to avoid mud puddles or deep holes that new mud puddles and deep holes are created, until eventually a whole network of false paths obscures the correct route. Stay alert and look beyond the worn spots to find where the trail picks up again. If you are uncertain about which path to take, try one for a short distance. If it seems to lead nowhere, turn around, go back to where you began, then start over. Don't compound a mistake by plunging farther and farther into the unknown.

In Hawai'i it is especially important to stay on trails—maybe more so than in other places—because thick undergrowth can mask deep cracks or overhangs and dense forest vegetation can obscure boundaries of private property. Many routes skirt or cross private property whose owners have granted hikers the right of way, but a *kapu* sign means no trespassing.

Pig and goat hunting are time-honored pastimes in the islands. At present, hunting is permitted in certain areas on weekends and holidays, but the schedule does change. Trailheads where hunting is allowed will usually have a sign saying so. If you stay on the trail and wear bright clothing, there is very little danger from hunters. Sticking to the trail will also help you respect cultural traditions by steering you away from religious sites and cemeteries.

Trailhead Vandalism

This is the most distressing, even if not life-threatening, experience most hikers ever face. For the most part, Hawaiians are friendly, helpful, and kind, but there are exceptions here as everywhere, and tourists are easy marks. Rental cars are usually obvious, and tourists are apt to leave all sorts of belongings in them when they go off for a hike.

If you are about to pull into a parking space at a remote trailhead and see broken glass on the ground, be warned.

Leave absolutely nothing in your car, not even in the trunk. Busy trailheads with people coming and going all day are usually safest. The odds against any unpleasant surprises are in your favor, but you can greatly improve them by taking a few precautions.

Zero Impact

We, as trail users, must be vigilant to make sure our passage leaves no lasting mark. Here are some basic guidelines for preserving trails in the region:

- Pack out all your own trash. You might also pack out garbage left by less-considerate hikers.
- Don't approach or feed any wild creatures—the bird eyeing your snack food is best able to survive if it remains self-reliant.
- Don't pick wildflowers or gather rocks, feathers, or other treasures along the trail. Removing these items will only take away from the next hiker's experience.
- Avoid damaging trailside soils and plants by remaining on the established route.
- Be courteous by not making loud noises while hiking.
- Many of these trails are multiuse, which means you'll share them with other hikers, trail runners, mountain bikers, and equestrians. Familiarize yourself with the proper trail etiquette, yielding the trail when appropriate.
- Use outhouses at trailheads or along the trail.

Three Zero-Impact Principles

- Leave with everything you brought in
- Leave no sign of your visit
- Leave the landscape as you found it

How to Use This Guide

To aid in decision making, each hike chapter begins with a quick summary that gives you a hint of the hiking adventure to follow. Next, you'll find the quick, nitty-gritty details of the hike: hike length, approximate hiking time, elevation gain, best hiking seasons, trail terrain, other trail users, trail contacts (for updates on trail conditions), canine compatibility, and trail usage fees.

The **Approximate hiking times** are based on a standard hiking pace of 1.5 to 2 miles per hour, adjusted for terrain and reflecting normal trail conditions. The stated times will get you there and back, but be sure to add time for rest breaks and enjoying the trail's attractions. Although the stated times offer a planning guideline, you should gain a sense of your personal health, capabilities, and hiking style and make this judgment for yourself. If you're hiking with a group, add enough time for slower members. The amount of carried gear also will influence hiking speed. In all cases leave enough daylight to accomplish the task safely.

The **Finding the trailhead** section gives you dependable directions from a nearby city or town right down to where you'll park your car. The hike description is the meat of the chapter. Detailed and honest, it's the author's carefully researched impression of the trail. While it's impossible to cover everything, you can rest assured that we won't miss what's important. In **Miles and Directions** we provide mileage cues to key junctions and trail name changes, as well as points of interest. The selected benchmarks allow for a quick check on progress and serve as your touchstone for staying on course.

How to Speak Hawaiian

The Hawaiian language has only twelve letters: the vowels a, e, i, o, and u, and the consonants h, k, l, m, n, p, and w. It also has a diacritical mark, the glottal stop (indicated by an apostrophe), that tells you how to separate the syllables. The apostrophe gives spoken Hawaiian its distinctive sound and rhythm. For example, chunky lava, *a'a,* is not pronounced "aaah," but "ah-ah." The word Hawai'i itself has a glottal stop, and you probably already know how to say it: "Howai-ee." If two vowels are not separated by a glottal stop, they are pronounced together, like the "ai" in Hawai'i.

Here are a few words you will hear over and over in Hawai'i. Many refer to physical features of the land and help interpret the names of significant landmarks:

a'a = rough, chunky lava
aloha = hello, good-by, love
heiau = holy place
kapu = taboo, forbidden, keep out
kea = white
kokua = please or help
loa = long
lua = hole or toilet
mahalo = thank you
makai = toward the sea
mauka = toward the mountain
mauna = mountain
pahoehoe = smooth, ropy lava
pali = cliff
pu'u = hill

Kaua'i Hike Ratings

All hikes in this guide are easy, but some are more strenuous than others. The list below rates hikes from easiest to most challenging.

Easiest

Most Challenging

Map Legend

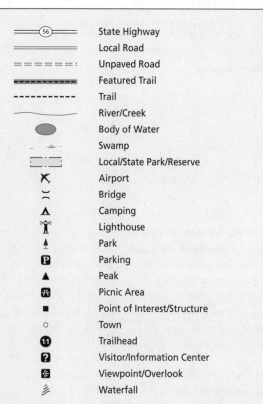

═══⟨56⟩═══	State Highway
═══════	Local Road
======:	Unpaved Road
▬▬▬▬▬▬	Featured Trail
- - - - - - -	Trail
~~	River/Creek
⬭	Body of Water
⸴⸴⸴	Swamp
▭▭▭	Local/State Park/Reserve
✕	Airport
⌣	Bridge
⛺	Camping
⛯	Lighthouse
⚘	Park
🅿	Parking
▲	Peak
⛘	Picnic Area
■	Point of Interest/Structure
○	Town
⓫	Trailhead
❓	Visitor/Information Center
⬕	Viewpoint/Overlook
⋛	Waterfall

1 Nounou Mountain (Sleeping Giant) East

The Sleeping Giant is the distinctive mountain behind Kapa'a and Wailua. The high (southernmost) point is his forehead; the next point to the north is his chin. The trail climbs up to his thighs and torso, makes a sharp turn, and goes up to his chest, where you can end the hike at a picnic spot or scramble all the way up to the summit. It offers great views and a good steady workout. It's popular with locals and tourists because it's so convenient to the Coconut Coast.

Distance: 3.2 miles out and back
Approximate hiking time: 2 to 3 hours
Elevation gain: 900 feet
Trail surface: Well-maintained lava with one or two eroded spots
Other trail users: None
Canine compatibility: Dogs permitted
Fees and permits: None
Seasons: Year-round
Land status: Nounou State Forest Reserve

Maps: *USGS Kapa'a; Kaua'i Recreational Trail Map* (Hawai'i Division of Forestry and Wildlife); *Northwestern Kaua'i Recreation Map* (Earthwalk Press)
Trail contact: Hawai'i Department of Land and Natural Resources; (808) 274-3433; www.hawaiitrails.org
Special considerations: Midday is hot so it's best to hike this trail in the morning and late afternoon.

Finding the trailhead: From the Lihue Airport, turn right (north) on HI 51, the first street after you leave the airport. In 1.5 miles HI 51 turns into HI 56 (the Kuhio Highway). Continue north for 4 more miles, crossing the Wailua River and passing the now abandoned Coco Palms Resort, to Haleilio Road at a traffic light. Turn west

Nounou Mountain (Sleeping Giant) East

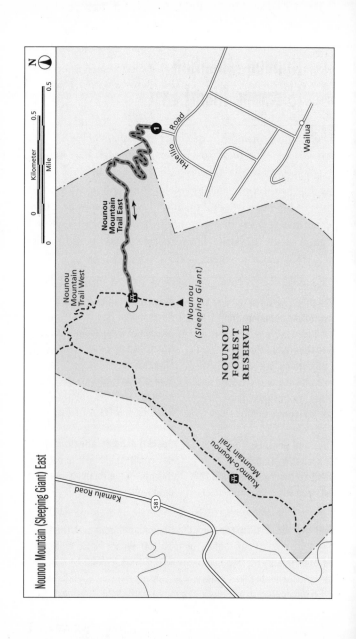

(*mauka*/toward the mountain) and drive a little over 1 mile to an inconspicuous parking area on the right. It's just before the road makes a turn to the left and is marked with a trail sign. **Trailhead GPS:** N22 03.40' / W159 20.46'

The Hike

The trail starts to the right (north) of the parking lot. Climb up a little ridge shaded by ironwood (big trees from Australia that look like pines but aren't). Before the climb gets serious, notice the small tree on the right with the succulent leaves covered in graffiti. It's called an autograph tree because writing on its leaves is more or less permanent. Begin a set of switchbacks lined with *koa haole* shrubs that shade the trail but block the cooling trade winds in exchange. The trail was originally marked every quarter mile, but only a few of these low metal markers remain.

The trail is clear and easy to follow except for a couple of scrambles over big rocks. You'll see lots of bare spots where hikers have cut the switchbacks, and in one or two places the way has become so badly eroded by shortcuts that it is hard to find. Please don't add to the damage.

After about 0.5 mile the grade levels out and even drops a bit, but not for long. The switchbacks resume and the trail swings south, climbing through strawberry guava to offer wonderful views of the jagged Anahola Mountains to the north. The route then crosses to the west side of the ridge to present equally fine views of the Makaleha Mountains to the west. After a few more switchbacks you come to a badly eroded red dirt patch. Go slowly here, keeping an eye out for the spot where the trail resumes, upward and to the right, then pause to notice how you got here so you won't get confused coming back down.

At 1.5 miles reach a junction with the Nounou Trail West coming in from the right (north). The sign is low and easy to miss. Turn right (north) and keep climbing, following a few more switchbacks to a flat grassy area with shaded, battered picnic tables. The Sleeping Giant's head is hidden from you here, as are the best views, but you can walk around the hilltop and peer through the foliage to find them. Enjoy the view and return the way you came.

Miles and Directions

0.0 Start at the Nounou Mountain East trailhead
1.5 Junction with Nounou Trail West; turn left (N22 03.49' / W159 21.14')
1.6 Picnic area
3.2 Return to trailhead

Option: You can continue another 0.3 mile to the very top of the giant's head, but the rest of the way is steep, requiring hands and feet now and then, and is dangerously slippery when wet. If you decide to continue, follow the trail down the far side of the grassy picnic area through a little dip, cross a narrow windy ridge, then scramble up a steep path—hardly a trail—to reach the giant's chin. Another narrow ridge and another short, steep grunt take you to the giant's head at 1,250 feet.

2 Kuamo'o-Nounou Mountain Trail

This pleasant ramble heads through forest along the western base of Nounou Mountain (the Sleeping Giant). You can stop (or turn around) at a covered picnic table overlooking the valley to the misty Makaleha Mountains, or continue to a junction with the Nounou Mountain Trail West. From there it's a steep 1-mile climb to the head of the Sleeping Giant as an option. There are a variety of native and introduced flowers to enjoy and wild fruits to eat along the hike, which is popular with locals.

Distance: 2.6 miles out and back

Approximate hiking time: 1 to 2 hours

Elevation gain: 300 feet

Trail surface: Fairly smooth well maintained lava

Other trail users: Cyclists and equestrians

Canine compatibility: Dogs permitted

Fees and permits: None

Seasons: Year-round

Land status: Nounou State Forest Reserve

Maps: USGS Kapa'a; Kaua'i Recreational Trail Map (Hawai'i Division of Forestry and Wildlife); Northwestern Kaua'i Recreation Map (Earthwalk Press)

Trail contact: Hawai'i Department of Land and Natural Resources; (808) 274-3433; www.hawaiitrails.org

Finding the trailhead: From the Lihue Airport turn right (north) onto HI 51. In 1.5 miles HI 51 turns into HI 56 (the Kuhio Highway). Continue north for 4 more miles. Just after the Wailua River crossing, turn left (mauka/toward the mountain) on HI 580 (Kuamo'o Road). Continue for 2.5 miles, passing the Opaeka'a Falls overlook. The trailhead is on the right (east) side of the road. It's easy to miss; there is only a small pullout for two to three cars, a small trailhead sign, and an open gate, painted yellow, at the edge of a field next to a house. **Trailhead GPS:** N22 03.00' / W159 21.59'

The Hike

Step over the threshold of the yellow gate and walk between private houses and pastureland on a mowed grass path. Drop down into a little gully to cross a creek on a bridge, then turn left (west) at a beautiful white-barked albizia tree. These big shady trees, with lacy-looking foliage and broad umbrella-shaped tops sprinkled with delicate white flowers, are especially pretty in spring and early summer. It's too bad they have become serious pests, crowding out native species.

The native *hau* thicket you'll pass through next has been able to hold its own against the invading albizia, however. Pass through another open gate and the dense hau forest gives way to dark overarching strawberry guava bushes, another invading species but one with edible fruit during the summer.

Climb another mile, up a rise, to a sheltered picnic table overlooking a valley. Pause to enjoy the view of the mountains beyond before retracing your steps to the trailhead.

Miles and Directions

0.0 Start Kuamo'o–Nounou trailhead

1.3 Picnic shelter

2.6 Return to trailhead

Option: If you want to climb another tough mile to the top of Nounou Mountain, follow the trail as it swings right (east) and rises and falls, veering right (east) again at a slightly obscure spot to pass a lonely clump of bamboo. Gradually

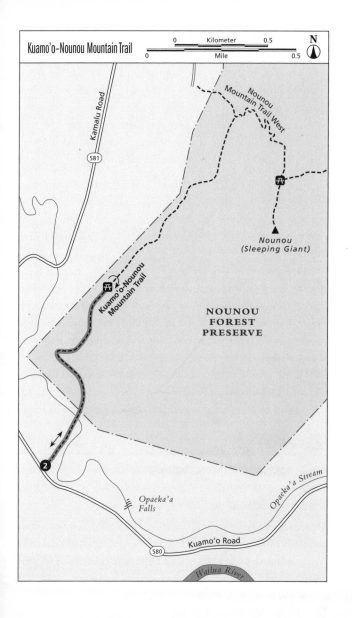

Kuamo'o-Nounou Mountain Trail

Kamalu Road

581

Nounou
Mountain Trail West

NOUNOU
FOREST
PRESERVE

Nounou
(Sleeping Giant)

Kuamo'o-Nounou
Mountain Trail

2

Opaeka'a
Falls

Opaeka'a Stream

Kuamo'o Road

580

Wailua River

0   Kilometer   0.5
0   Mile   0.5

gain altitude by way of a few switchbacks as you pass in and out of streambeds decorated with an assortment of ferns, reaching the highest point on the trail (640 feet) amid a grove of Norfolk Island pines. A clearing here offers another vista. After crossing a few more gullies meet the Nounou Mountain Trail West, where you turn right (south) and head steeply uphill to the summit of Nounou Mountain. The left (west) fork takes you back out into the suburbs and to the Nounou Mountain West trailhead.

3 Keahua Forestry Arboretum

This lovely, tranquil spot is perfect for a quiet stroll, a picnic, and a dip in a stream in the cooler uplands above Lihue. It was originally planned as an outdoor nature classroom by the Kaua'i forestry department, planted with scattered clumps of native and introduced trees that attract a variety of birds. It is near the trailheads for two popular trails, the easy and very popular Kuilau Ridge Trail and the long and rigorous Powerline Trail.

Distance: 0.5 mile out and back
Approximate hiking time: 20 to 30 minutes
Elevation gain: 50 feet
Trail surface: Grass and gravel path
Other trail users: Horses and cyclists
Canine compatibility: Dogs not permitted
Fees and permits: None

Seasons: Year-round
Land status: Lihue-Koloa Forest Reserve
Maps: *USGS Wai'ale'ale; Kaua'i Recreational Trail Map* (Hawai'i Division of Forestry and Wildlife)
Trail contact: Hawai'i Department of Land and Natural Resources; (808) 273-3433; www.hawaiitrails.org

Finding the trailhead: From the Lihue Airport turn right (north) onto HI 51. In 1.5 miles HI 51 turns into HI 56 (the Kuhio Highway). Continue north for another 4 miles. Just after the Wailua River crossing, turn left (*mauka*/toward the mountain) on HI 580 (Kuamo'o Road). Continue on this ever-narrowing road, through suburbs and semirural land, for about 7 miles to the arboretum. Keahua Stream runs through the center, right across the road. It's quite shallow except in heavy rain, and you can park on either side of it. The road does continue on beyond the stream, but it's only passable for four-wheel-drive vehicles. **Trailhead GPS:** N22 04.15' / W159 25.10'

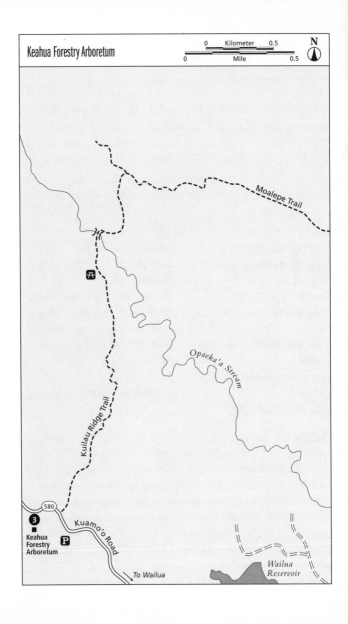

Keahua Forestry Arboretum

N

0   Kilometer   0.5

0   Mile   0.5

Moalepe Trail

Opaeka'a Stream

Kuilau Ridge Trail

580

3
Keahua
Forestry
Arboretum

P

Kuamo'o Road

To Wailua

Wailua
Reservoir

The Hike

Head left (south) up the grassy hill on a little path that begins on the far (west) side of the stream, climbing past a small grove of eucalyptus trees called painted gums. Their smooth trunks are beautifully streaked and striped in the most delicate of grays, pinks, greens, and oranges. Giant African tulip trees with great red flower heads that bloom almost year-round are scattered here and there over the grounds. There are birds everywhere: Brazilian red-crested cardinals, perky little gray and white birds with bright red heads and red crests sticking up; the ubiquitous mynahs; cattle egrets; shama thrushes; several kinds of doves; and, of course, the ever-present Kaua'i jungle fowl.

In not much more than 100 yards, veer left (southeast) and climb a little knoll to a covered picnic table near a patch of *hala* to enjoy the quiet. From here you can drop back down the slope, cross the stream to the east side, and admire the big white-barked albizia tree draped in a cloak of escaped philodendrons, the same plants you're likely to see at the dentist's office. In the congenial Hawaiian climate they run rampant. You'll also pass a little patch of papyrus, like upside-down feather dusters along the water's edge, as well as a row of guava and *kukui* trees, the state tree of Hawai'i. Along the eastern edge of the park is a patch of *hau*, a shrub whose branches are so dense and tangled you will wonder "hau" to get through it. It's a kind of hibiscus, with striking yellow flowers with dark purple-brown centers. At the top of this slope are two big mango trees shading another picnic table. There's a fairly deep pool beneath the mangoes, one of which has a rope attached for swinging out over the stream. Wander as long as you like, then return to your car.

4 Kuilau Ridge Trail

The scenery on this hike is drop-dead gorgeous, and since the entire hike is on an old road, you can actually enjoy it while you're walking without slipping on tree roots or falling over slimy rocks. You can combine this hike with the Moalepe Trail, and many people do, but you need to have a ride at the other end, or be prepared to turn around and come back the same way. If you have time to do only one of the two hikes, this one is the more interesting. When you've finished, you can have a quick dip in the stream to cool off at the Keahua Forestry Arboretum, just around the corner.

Distance: 4 miles out and back
Approximate hiking time: 2 to 3 hours
Elevation gain: 740 feet
Trail surface: Abandoned road
Other trail users: Cyclists and horses
Canine compatibility: Leashed dogs permitted
Fees and permits: None
Seasons: Year-round, but muddy in winter
Land status: Lihue-Koloa State Forest Reserve

Maps: USGS Wai'ale'ale, Kapa'a
Trail contact: Hawai'i Department of Land and Natural Resources; (808) 274-3433; www.hawaiitrails.org
Special considerations: Judging from the broken glass often seen at this trailhead, this is a likely spot for your car to be broken into. Leave nothing in your vehicle—or better yet, park at the Keahua Forestry Arboretum, which is not quite so isolated.

Finding the trailhead: From the Lihue airport drive north on HI 56 (the Kuhio Highway) to HI 580 (the Kuamo'o Road) in Wailua, just beyond the Wailua River. Turn left (*mauka*/toward the mountain) and continue uphill through suburbs and semirural areas on the narrowing road for about 7 miles to the marked trailhead on the right (north). If you reach the arboretum you've gone too far. Four or five cars can be parked at the trailhead; no facilities. **Trailhead GPS: N22 04.16' / W159 24.59'**

The Hike

A good map is posted at the trailhead, along with information about how to avoid contributing to the spread of an especially noxious weed called purple plague. There is also a place to brush off your boots before and after your hike to remove any hitchhiking seeds you might have picked up. This plant is a serious bad guy.

Walk up the smooth well-graded road, ascending gently at first, slightly more steeply later, but never strenuously. There are mileage signs almost every 0.25 mile. The way is lined with paperbark trees, guavas, *kukui* nuts, and all kinds of ferns and vines and creepers. One especially beautiful vine is a wild sweet potato with perfectly heart-shaped leaves.

As you gain elevation you get better and better views of the Makaleha Mountains, whose tops are almost always obscured by clouds. Among the peaks are Mount Wai'ale'ale, said to be the wettest spot on earth, and Mount Kawaikini (5,243 feet), highest point on Kaua'i. You can usually see back down the valley all the way to the beach where the Wailua River flows into the sea. You also get a good look at Nounou, the Sleeping Giant, whose slopes also offer several good hikes. All around you are patches of green in an unimaginable variety of colors and textures. In the higher elevations you also see fewer weeds and more Hawaiian natives, such as *ohia lehua* with its bright red powder-puff flowers.

At 1.25 miles you'll reach a flat mowed picnic area with sheltered picnic tables and spectacular views in all directions.

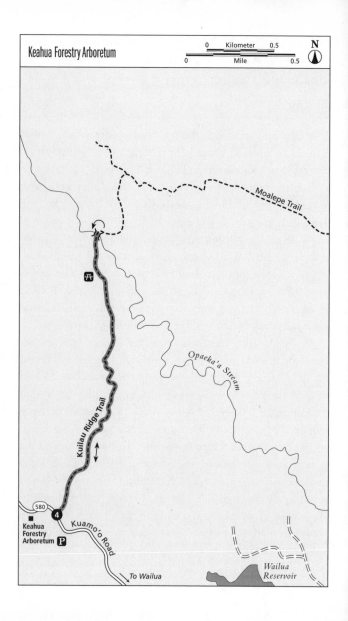

Keahua Forestry Arboretum

Kilometer

Mile

N

Moalepe Trail

Opaeka'a Stream

Kuilau Ridge Trail

580

4

Kuamo'o Road

Keahua
Forestry
Arboretum

P

To Wailua

Wailua
Reservoir

This is the high point of your hike at 1,140 feet. From here, the trail drops down to the northeast a bit, winds around a ridge, rises a bit, and arrives at a bridge over Opaeka'a Stream. This is the official end of the Kuilau Trail, as a sign will tell you, and is also the end of the Moalepe Trail, coming up from the other side of the mountain. You can turn around and go back to your car from here or continue another 2.75 miles down to the Moalepe trailhead.

Miles and Directions

- **0.0** Start from the trailhead
- **1.2** High point at 1,140 feet
- **2.0** Bridge and end of trail (N22 05.30' / W159 24.44')
- **4.0** Return to trailhead

5 Moalepe Trail

This trail meets the Kuilau Ridge Trail just below a ridgetop. Since the two trails come together at one spot, it is a mystery why they are not considered one and the same. At any rate, you can hike this one to the junction then turn around, or it can be combined with the Kuilau Ridge route for a longer hike. The Moalepe Trail is less heavily traveled and gives you a different, and perhaps more dramatic view of the Makahela Mountains. You will need a car shuttle unless you don't mind walking all the way back. If you have to choose between the two routes, the Kuilau trail is more scenic.

Distance: 5.4 miles out and back

Approximate hiking time: 2 to 3 hours

Elevation gain: 680 feet

Trail surface: Mostly abandoned road

Other trail users: Bicyclists and equestrians

Canine compatibility: Leashed dogs permitted

Fees and permits: None

Seasons: Year-round, but may be muddy in winter

Land status: Lihue-Koloa State Forest Reserve

Maps: *USGS Kapa'a* and *Wai'ale'ale*

Trail contact: Hawai'i Department of Land and Natural Resources; (808) 274-3433; www.hawaiitrails.org

Finding the trailhead: From the Lihue airport drive north on HI 56 (the Kuhio Highway) to HI 580 (the Kuamo'o Road) in Wailua, just beyond the Wailua River. Turn left (*mauka*/toward the mountain) on HI 580, and in 3 miles right (north) on HI 581. Continue 1.5 miles to Olohena Road, turn left (*mauka*/toward the mountain) and drive 1.5 miles to where the road makes a sharp right turn and becomes Waipouli Road. Park at a wide spot on the roadside. The trailhead

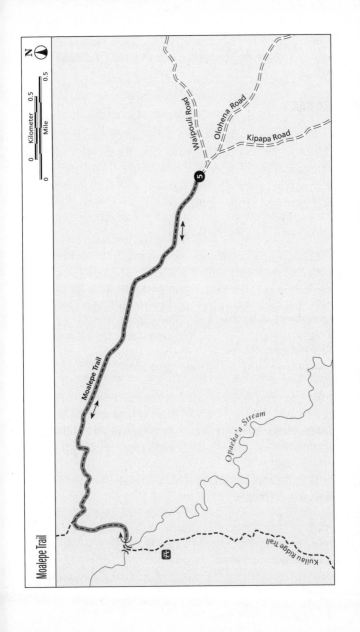

Moalepe Trail

N

Waipouli Road

Olohena Road

Kipapa Road

5

Moalepe Trail

Opaeka'a Stream

Kuilau Ridge Trail

Kilometer   0.5   0.5

Mile   0.5

is well marked with a brown and gold sign. Do not leave anything
in your car. There are no amenities at the trailhead. **Trailhead GPS:**
N22 04.59' / W159 23.03'

The Hike

Head east on a road through a fenced pasture that climbs
almost imperceptibly for 1 mile. The shrubs with soft gray
foliage and pretty pink flowers beside the trail are downy
rose myrtle, unfortunately invasive weeds. You will also
find guavas to eat along the way.

The trail then narrows a little and climbs more steeply,
heading directly toward the Makaleha Mountains. There are
beautiful views down into the valley to the left (south) as
well. Pass through a tunnel of shaggy paperbark trees, make
one last short climb to an open spot, then descend a couple
of switchbacks into the Opaeka'a Stream valley and a little
bridge with a sign marking the ends of the Moalepe and
Kuilau Ridge trails.

From here you can return the way you came, or continue on the Kuilau Ridge Trail for another 2 miles to the
Kuilau Ridge trailhead. This is a shuttle option, or you can
hike to the trailhead and then all the way back, as many
locals do (10 miles round-trip). You also can continue on
up the trail for another few minutes to a picnic area with
covered tables.

Miles and Directions

0.0 Start

2.7 End at bridge (N22 05.70' / W159 24.44')

5.4 Return to trailhead

6 Kapa'a Shoreline Trail

This hike follows a section of the new Ke Ala Hele Maka-lae (The Path that Goes by the Coast) hiking/biking route which, when completed, will run all the way from Lihue to Anahola, halfway up Kauai's eastern coast. It is so new that some sections have not been opened, but the part described here is especially rewarding and is already getting lots of use. It is smoothly paved—even wheelchair-accessible—and follows closely along the shoreline past some of Kauai's finest public beaches and windblown sea cliffs. Handsome iron railings decorated with sugarcane and pineapple motifs line the exposed sections of trail, as well as the bridges that cross several canals and streams that would make it otherwise impossible to proceed very far this close to the shore. You can go as long as you like.

Distance: 7 miles out and back
Approximate hiking time: 2 to 4 hours
Elevation change: Negligible
Trail surface: Cement and asphalt
Other trail users: Cyclists and skaters
Canine compatibility: Dogs are permitted only on certain sections of the path. They must be on leashes and owners must carry poop bags.
Fees and permits: None
Seasons: Year-round
Land status: State park, county parks, and private right-of-way through Kealia Kai
Maps: *USGS Kapa'a*, but no map is really needed
Trail contact: Hawai'i Department of Parks and Recreation; (808) 274-3444; www.kauai path.org/kauaicoastalpath

Finding the trailhead: From Lihue drive north of HI 56 (the Kuhio Highway) to the town of Kapa'a. Turn right (*makai/*toward the sea) onto Panihi Road. If you reach Kaloloku Road, with a Shell gas station, a Burger King, and a Seventh-day Adventist Church, you've gone too far. Drive a short distance to where the road ends and turn left (north) on the narrow lane that parallels the shore. The lane ends at a small parking and picnic area. Do not leave anything in your car. There are bathrooms, water, and lifeguards, as well as access to the highway, at the larger county beach parks along the route. **Trailhead GPS:** N22 04.11' / W159 19.03'

The Hike

The signed biking/hiking trail begins to the right (north) at a new bridge arching over the Waikaea Canal. Cross the bridge and follow the smooth path along the shore to Kapa'a Beach, broad, sandy, and popular with snorkelers. The sand pinches out and the crowds disappear after about 1 mile, where the path meanders along a cliff above a section of undeveloped shoreline. Little rest pavilions located at intervals along the route, with covered benches and places to park bicycles, offer you the chance to step out of the way of other travelers on the main path and gaze out over the sea.

At 1.8 miles a little hill cuts you off from the sea breeze for a few minutes before the prospect opens up again and you cross a bridge over Kapa'a Stream onto Kealia Beach, another big, busy park with lifeguard stations and other facilities. At the far end of this beach the sand pinches out once again and the path clings to the side of a cliff as it rounds a windy corner. This section passes the Kealia Kai development, which is private property, so stay on the trail.

Pass an overgrown old cemetery and a *heiau* (religious site) on the right (do not disturb), before arriving at an

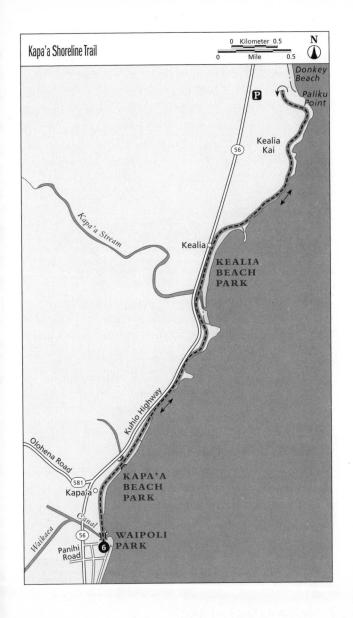

Kapa'a Shoreline Trail

0   Kilometer   0.5

0   Mile   0.5

N

Donkey
Beach

Paliku
Point

P

Kealia
Kai

56

Kapa'a Stream

Kealia

KEALIA
BEACH
PARK

Kuhio Highway

Olohena Road

581

Kapa'a

KAPA'A
BEACH
PARK

Canal

56

Waikaea

Panihi
Road

6 WAIPOLI
PARK

especially scenic rest pavilion overlooking idyllic little Kuna Bay, known locally as Donkey Beach. It is usually not crowded since it is not visible from the highway. Continue downhill another 0.1 mile to a spot at a break in a fence on the *mauka* (left) side of the trail, where a path (also paved) meets yours. This is the turnaround point, though you may wish to follow one of the dirt paths on the right *(makai)* down to the little bay. From here, retrace your steps to the trailhead.

Miles and Directions

0.0 Trailhead and beginning of bike path. Turn right (north) onto the path.

1.8 Bridge over Kapa'a Stream at Kealia Beach Park (N22 05.38' / W159 18.27')

3.5 Turnaround point at bottom of a trail leading up to HI 56 (N22 06.27' / W159 17.50')

7.0 Return to the trailhead.

Option: If you would like to do this hike as a one-way shuttle hike, turn left *(mauka)* at the paved junction at 3.5 miles, where an unmarked trail meets yours. Head uphill through tall shrubbery to a parking lot off HI 56 where you can leave one vehicle. The parking lot is isolated and maybe not the best place to leave a car for too long, but there is a bathroom there.

7 Kilauea Lighthouse

Officially named Kilauea Point National Wildlife Refuge, this is a birdwatcher's paradise, as well as a very likely place to see dolphins, turtles, rare monk seals, and even whales. The historic lighthouse on the point and the lovely views up the north shore are irresistible to photographers. There are interpretive exhibits, docents on duty to answer questions, and of course, there's a gift shop.

Distance: 0.5-mile loop
Approximate hiking time: 40 minutes, but you can spend several hours on the point
Elevation change: None
Trail surface: Paved
Other trail users: None
Canine compatibility: Dogs not permitted
Fees and permits: A national refuge fee is charged.

Seasons: Year-round; whales present Dec–Apr
Schedule: Open daily from 10:00 a.m. to 4:00 p.m.
Land status: Kilauea Point National Wildlife Refuge
Maps: *USGS Anahola*, but no map is needed
Trail contact: Kaua'i National Wildlife Refuge Complex; (808) 828-1413; www.kilaueapoint.org

Finding the trailhead: From Lihue drive north on HI 56 for about 26 miles to Kilauea. Turn right (*makai*/toward the sea) onto Kolo Street at the Shell gas station. Turn left (northeast) at the very first block onto Kilauea Road and follow it for 1 mile, passing a scenic overlook on the right (east). Drive through the gate (no pedestrians allowed), downhill to a parking area, just beyond which you will find the refuge entrance kiosk. There are bathrooms near the entrance.
Trailhead GPS: N22 13.45' / W159 24.09'

The Hike

You'll probably be greeted in the parking lot by a *nene*—one of Hawaii's rare geese—or two. Do not feed them. Pick up a brochure as you go through the entrance kiosk to help you identify the refuge birds, when to see them nesting, and when and where to watch for sea mammals.

The paved path skirts the edge of the long point, out around the lighthouse in a counterclockwise direction and back again. Near the beginning, look back to the right (east) toward the ironwood trees on the hillside across the little bay. The trees are almost obscured by the bodies of thousands of birds perched among the branches, including red-footed boobies and cattle egrets. Red-tailed and white-tailed tropic birds sometimes sweep past the cliff so closely you can almost touch them. Shearwaters, petrels, and black, prehistoric-looking frigate birds soar overhead, and in winter and early spring Laysan albatross calmly nest in hollows on the hillside only a few feet away from you.

Don't forget to look for monk seals sunning themselves among the rocks in the bay. They are the same color and smooth texture as the boulders and they don't move much, so they are easy to miss.

The paved path that follows the cliff edge is lined with *naupaka* and other Hawaiian native plants. *Naupaka (Scaevola* spp.) is a succulent large-leaved shrub with peculiar white flowers that look like they have been torn in half. They are not mutants or damaged however; their lopsided shape is an adaptation for pollinators.

There are several versions of a Hawaiian myth that explains how they lost their other halves. In one account *naupaka* flowers were once whole, but a beautiful maiden

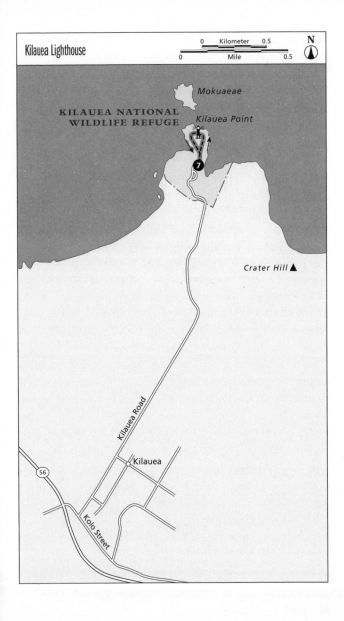

Kilauea Lighthouse

0   Kilometer   0.5

0   Mile   0.5

N

Mokuaeae

KILAUEA NATIONAL
WILDLIFE REFUGE

Kilauea Point

7

Crater Hill ▲

Kilauea Road

56

Kilauea

Kolo Street

(it's *always* a beautiful maiden) unfairly accused her lover of being unfaithful, and in her anger tore a flower in half and told him she would not trust him or speak to him again until he brought her a new, whole one. To punish her the gods turned all *naupaka* flowers into halves, and the boy died of a broken heart.

There are both mountain species and beach species of *naupaka,* and another myth has to do with a maiden on a beach being separated from her lover on a mountain, and the gods turning each into a half flower symbolizing their loneliness and grief.

You can examine the little lighthouse near the point up close and check out the exhibits in the structure behind it before returning to the parking lot.

8 Upper Powerline Trail

The Powerline Trail runs a slippery swath from Princeville up into the Makaleha Mountains and down again to the Keahua Forestry Arboretum not far from Kapa'a. It's an old road that does indeed follow a string of power lines, much of it along a ridge that would be scenic if it weren't so over-grown. There are some spectacular views now and then, though. Since it does run right up over the mountains it is wet most of the time, with deep puddles that inundate the road/trail from one side to the other. The entire trail is 13 miles long and the going is slow. It takes an exhausting long day to do it all, but you don't have to. This hike gives you just a taste of the trail, at its northern, easier end. This hike covers the first 2 miles and back, but you can go farther if you like.

Distance: 4 miles out and back
Approximate hiking time: 2 to 3 hours
Elevation gain: About 700 feet
Trail surface: Badly eroded road; slick and muddy
Other trail users: Mountain bikers, equestrians, and motorcyclists
Seasons: Avoid the trail in winter or any time it has been raining long and steadily
Canine compatibility: Dogs are allowed on leash, but if you have a small dog, it had better have long legs or be a good swimmer
Fees and permits: None
Land status: Halelea Forest Reserve
Maps: *USGS Hanalei*
Trail contact: Hawai'i Department of Land and Natural Resources; (808) 274-3433; www.hawaiitrails.org.
Special considerations: The route is popular with hunters. Wear bright clothing.

Finding the trailhead: From the Lihue Airport drive north on HI 56 (the Kuhio Highway) for 30 miles to the Princeville Airport. About 1 mile beyond the end of the airport look for a horse cutout sign advertising the Princeville Ranch Stables. This is Po'oku Road. Turn left (*mauka*/toward the mountain) and drive less than 2 miles to the trailhead. **Trailhead GPS:** N22 11.03' / W159 27.25'

The Hike

The walk begins beside two big water tanks on a deceptively wide, smooth, level road. You can see the power lines running up the mountain. There is a hunter's checkpoint station at the trailhead plastered with notices of lost dogs. You'll see why soon.

The road climbs gently but steadily between tall grasses, tangles of *hau,* guavas, and Java plum up a ridge above the Hanalei River. Most of the time the vegetation is too dense for views, but in some spots it thins out and gives you a sighting of the green Hanalei valley, the pointy peak of Mount Hihimanu, and at least one waterfall—more if it has been raining. Whenever you detour to find a viewpoint be very careful and watch your feet in the dense foliage since you might not realize that you are teetering on a sheer cliff edge or even an overhang. Among the trees and shrubs along the trail, purple Philippine ground orchids and purple and white bamboo orchids with bamboo-like stalks contribute spots of color to the green and the mist.

The road becomes steeper as you go; the ruts and the puddles deeper. You'll be busy looking for the highest, driest, least slippery ground, and won't have time for views after the first 1.5 miles. But if you continue to struggle for another 0.2 mile the grade lessens and the road begins to look a little more like a road again. By the time you have

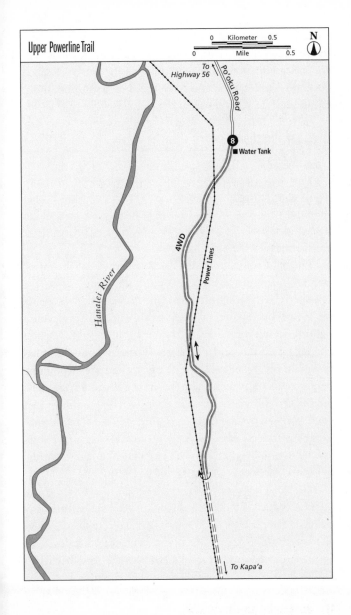

Upper Powerline Trail

0   Kilometer   0.5
0   Mile   0.5

N

To
Highway 56

Poʻoku Road

8 ■ Water Tank

4WD

Power Lines

Hanalei River

To Kapaʻa

gone 2 miles you will have seen what the Powerline Trail is like and will probably be ready to turn around—though you can continue for 11 more miles all the way to Keahua Forestry Arboretum if you have the time and the stamina. Otherwise, retrace your steps to your car.

Miles and Directions

0.0   Trailhead
2.0   Turnaround point (N22 09.50' / W159 27.39')
4.0   Return to trailhead

⑨ Limahuli Garden and Preserve

This wonderful garden beneath the cliffs of the Na Pali Coast is one of five national tropical botanical gardens in Hawai'i, chartered by Congress in 1976 to promote research and education and to preserve ecosystems and cultural knowledge. It's a good place to learn about some of the things you'll see along Kauai's trails and roadsides—not just their names, but their uses and the Hawaiian myths and legends associated with them. A loop trail winds through a beautiful setting along Limahuli Stream, with some photogenic ocean views as backdrops to the flowers. The garden has a collection of extremely rare species, some of which are almost extinct in the wild, the most interesting of which is the celebrated Brighamia, the bizarre "cabbage on a baseball bat."

Distance: 0.8-mile loop

Approximate hiking time: 1 hour or less

Elevation gain: 200 feet

Trail surface: Smooth easy gravel or pavement

Other trail users: None

Canine compatibility: Dogs not permitted

Fees and permits: The entry fee includes an illustrated booklet worth the price of admission.

Private tours available.

Schedule: Open daily, except Mon and Sat, from 9:30 a.m. to 4:00 p.m.

Seasons: Year-round

Land status: Private

Maps: USGS Ha'ena, but the one at the back of the garden booklet is the one to use

Trail contact: National Tropical Botanical Gardens (Hawai'i); (808) 826-1053; www.ntbg.org

Finding the trailhead: From Lihue follow HI 56 (the Kuhio Highway), which becomes HI 560 in Hanalei 39 miles farther, almost to its end. The garden is on the left (*mauka*/toward the mountain) side

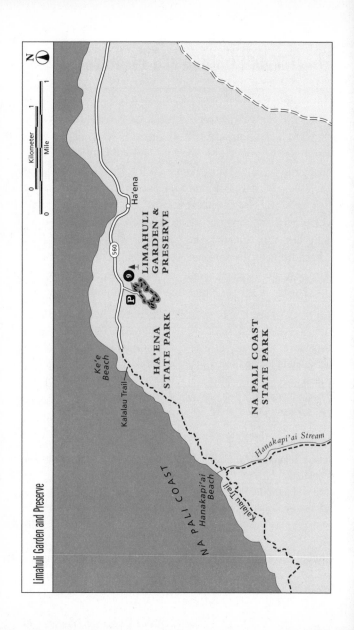

Limahuli Garden and Preserve

N

0   Kilometer   1
0   Mile   1

Ha'ena

560

LIMAHULI
GARDEN &
PRESERVE

P

9

Ke'e
Beach

Kalalau Trail

HA'ENA
STATE PARK

N A   P A L I   C O A S T

Hanakapi'ai Beach

Kalalau Trail

NA PALI
COAST STATE
PARK

Hanakapi'ai Stream

of the road, just before Ha'ena State Park. The garden has a parking lot away from the crowds below and protected from vandalism. Restrooms and water at the visitor center. **Trailhead GPS** (approximate): N22 13.10' / W159 34.31'

The Hike

The walk starts beneath a beautiful big breadfruit tree in front of the visitor center, then wanders up along Limahuli Stream, through terraces planted with taro and other plants used by the early (and some contemporary) Hawaiians. Part of the walk passes through native Hawaiian forest, and another section is devoted to threatened species, of which Hawai'i has more than its share.

There is a separate section of introduced species, with information about how they got to Hawai'i. You might be surprised to learn that bananas, coconuts, mangos, guava, and sugarcane, among others, are not native Hawaiian plants at all, but were brought here by the early Hawaiians for use as food, medicine, and tools, or as ornamental plantings introduced by later immigrants from Asia, Europe, and the Americas. There is a re-creation of a typical garden from the sugar plantation era, and an archeological site has been preserved at the upper end of the garden.

The loop trail brings you back to the visitor center where you began.

10 Ke'e Beach-Kalalau Overlook

This very popular short, though rugged, hike gives you a sample of the Kalalau Trail along the famous Na Pali Coast. The entire Kalalau Trail follows the windward coast for 11 challenging miles to its end at Kalalau Beach, but you can experience a bit of it without too much effort. The glorious views begin almost as soon as you start the climb above Ke'e Beach, with its classic turquoise bay wreathed with tropical foliage and flowers. The overlook at the end of the hike reveals the long Na Pali coastline, lying at the base of some of the sharpest, most vertical, most dramatically beautiful cliffs in the world.

Distance: 1 mile out and back
Approximate hiking time: 1 hour
Elevation gain: 250 feet
Trail surface: Rocky, muddy, and slippery natural surface
Other trail users: None
Canine compatibility: Dogs on leash permitted
Fees and permits: None
Seasons: Spring, summer, fall
Land status: Na Pali Coast State Wilderness Park, Ha'ena State Park

Maps: USGS Ha'ena; Northwestern Kaua'i Recreation Map (Earthwalk Press)
Trail contact: Hawai'i Division of State Parks; (808) 274-3444; www.hawaiistateparks.org
Special considerations: This trail is steep and slippery when wet, and it rains a lot here. Wear good shoes and old clothes, and carry water.

Finding the trailhead: From Lihue drive HI 56 (the Kuhio Highway), which becomes HI 560 at Hanalei, for 41 miles, all the way to its end at Ha'ena State Park. The trailhead is across the street on the left (west). There is a parking lot and some space on the street, but it fills up early. Restrooms and water are near the parking area. **Trailhead GPS:** N22 13.13' / W159 34.58'

The Hike

The hike begins on the left (west) side of the road at a rain shelter where muddy hikers who have just finished the trail wait for rides or for slower companions to catch up. You immediately begin a slippery, rocky climb that gives you a taste of how rough a hike the entire 22-mile round trip expedition can be (especially with a backpack). Take your time and stop frequently to enjoy the scenery.

It often rains here, but you probably won't mind a cooling shower as you labor up the slope. The trail is shaded by *hala* trees with their peculiar stilt roots; their spirally arranged leaves are used all over the South Pacific to make everything from hats to floor mats. The female plants have big bumpy fruits that are sometimes called tourist pineapples since they do resemble pineapples, though they are not even remotely related and are definitely not good to eat. You will also see lots of ironwood, the tree that looks like a pine but is not. It comes from Australia.

As you climb, be sure to look away from your feet back down onto Ke'e Beach behind you, which becomes more spectacular at every turn with its blue water and white sand—everybody's daydream of paradise.

In about 0.5 mile you will reach a high point where the view up the coastline to the north is probably one of the most famous in the world. It is extremely windy at this point, so hang onto your headgear. There must be a huge pile of hats and visors at the base of the cliff, snatched away from hikers' heads by sudden gusts.

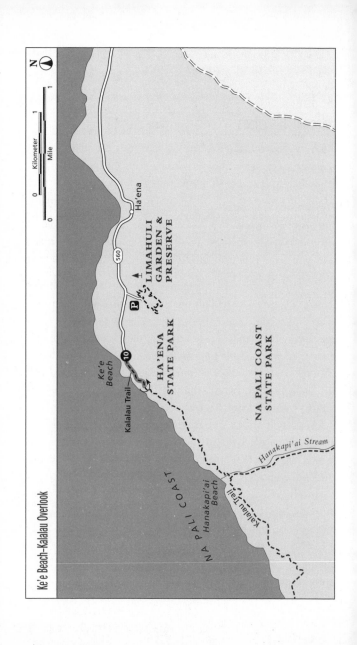

Ke'e Beach-Kalalau Overlook

N

0   Kilometer   1
0   Mile   1

Ke'e
Beach

Ha'ena

560

LIMAHULI
GARDEN &
PRESERVE

P

Kalalau Trail

10

HA'ENA
STATE PARK

NA PALI COAST

Hanakapi'ai Beach

Kalalau Trail

Hanakapi'ai Stream

NA PALI COAST
STATE PARK

This is the turnaround point of your hike. Enjoy the views, then retrace your steps carefully back down the muddy path to your car.

Miles and Directions

- **0.0** Kalalau Trailhead
- **0.5** Overlook (N22 13.05' / W159 35.13')
- **1.0** Return to trailhead

Option: It is possible to continue another 1.5 miles to Hanakapi'ai Beach, but you can't go beyond that point without a wilderness permit. If you decide to go on, make sure you have plenty of water and be advised that the rest of the way is downhill, so you will have to climb back up on your return.

11 Kukuiolono Park

This hike isn't exactly a wilderness experience, but there isn't much wilderness left in the golf course/resort region of Kaua'i. You can get a nice hike in anyway, circling two jogging paths of about 0.5-mile each, visiting a tiny Japanese garden, then following a walkway that goes right through the middle of the golf course to a pavilion on a hill overlooking the ocean.

Distance: 2.2 miles; two loops plus out-and-back
Approximate hiking time: 1 to 1.5 hours
Elevation gain: 50 feet
Trail surface: Grass, asphalt, gravel path
Other trail users: None, except an occasional golf cart in one area
Canine compatibility: Dogs on leash permitted

Fees and permits: None
Schedule: 7:00 a.m. to 6:30 p.m.
Seasons: Year-round
Land status: County park
Maps: *USGS Koloa,* but you don't really need a map
Trail contact: Hawai'i Department of Parks and Recreation; (808) 332-9151. www.recreation .parks.net

Finding the trailhead: From the Lihue Airport take HI 50 (the Kaumualii Highway) south, then west, to Kalaheo. Turn left (*makai/* toward the sea) on Papalina Road. In a little more than 1 mile watch for the KUKUIOLONO PARK AND GOLF COURSE sign on the right (west). Turn in under the stone arch and park on the right (north). **Trailhead GPS:** N21 91.21' / W159 53.05'

The Hike

The first loop, south of the access road, begins at the parking lot, heading west (counterclockwise) on a wide shady path under ironwood, Brazilian pepper, and eucalyptus trees. It makes an irregular oval, rising and falling gently and returns to the parking area.

The second loop begins right across the road from the first at a sign prohibiting horses and motor vehicles. You will also see another path going off to the left (east). This second circuit is a little shorter than the first one, but maybe more interesting. You go down (clockwise) into a dip lined with grass growing higher than your head, then through a corridor of tall trees almost completely obscured by a dense drapery of yellow-flowered trumpet vines, a dazzling Niagara of green and gold that will stop you in your tracks. Just beyond, the trees whose canopies have not been smothered are being invaded from the other direction with oversized philodendrons climbing up their trunks.

When this second circuit brings you back to the parking area, turn left (south) and follow the park road about 0.25 mile (you can even get back in your car and drive it if you want to) to a second parking area beyond some stone carvings. From here an asphalt path extends south from the parking lot to the right of a sign that says HAWAIIANA EXHIBIT where, tucked behind a hedge, a pretty little Japanese garden is planted with *ti*, ferns, begonias, palms, and orange trees, and threaded with a gravel "stream" spanned with miniature bridges. Walk a few paces back to the parking area and follow the other paved path that heads south-

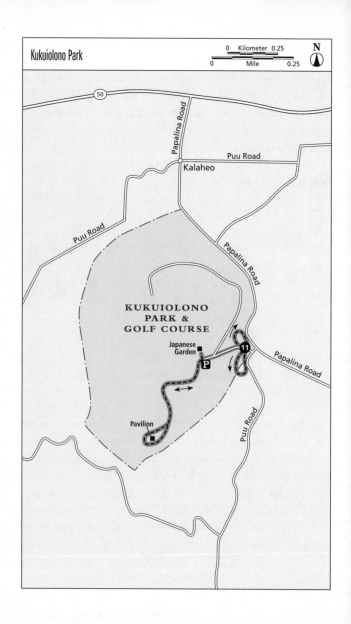

Kukuiolono Park

0   Kilometer 0.25
0   Mile   0.25

N

50

Papalina Road

Puu Road

Kalaheo

Puu Road

Papalina Road

KUKUIOLONO
PARK
&
GOLF COURSE

Japanese
Garden

P

11

Papalina Road

Puu Road

Pavilion

east, stepping over a low chain gate. This one takes you past a neatly planted patch of plumeria trees and out across the golf course to a green painted pavilion consisting of a covered picnic area and bathrooms. There is a pleasant view out over the ocean in one direction and the Hoary Head (or Haupu) Mountains in another. From here, retrace your steps to the parking lot.

Miles and Directions

- **0.0** Parking area at park entrance
- **0.5** Return to parking area after circling the first loop
- **1.0** Return to parking area after circling the second loop
- **1.2** Follow the park road south to the second parking area and Japanese garden
- **1.6** Follow the path southeast through the golf course to the pavilion (N21 90.86' / W159 52.47')
- **2.2** Return to first parking area at park entrance

12 Russian Fort Elizabeth

Russian Fort Elizabeth State Historical Park is the site of a little known and surprising slice of Hawaiian history. The town of Waimea was a major port in the 1800s, a time when Russia, represented by the Russian-American Company, needed a stopover for ships carrying supplies to fur trappers and traders in Alaska. In 1815 it sent George Schaeffer to forge an alliance with King Kaumuali'i of Kaua'i to build a fort at Waimea in exchange for helping Kaumuali'i to overthrow King Kamehameha I. The fort was begun, and named Fort Elizabeth in honor of the czarina, but the Americans soon saw to it that Schaeffer was evicted, and the Russians never came. There isn't much left but the outer walls because the fort was dismantled in 1864, but there is an interpretive panel to help you picture it as it was.

Distance: 0.5-mile lollipop
Approximate hiking time: 20 to 30 minutes
Elevation gain: None
Trail surface: Grass and gravel path
Other trail users: None
Canine compatibility: Dogs on leash permitted
Fees and permits: None
Schedule: Daily during daylight
Seasons: Year-round

Land status: Russian Fort Elizabeth State Historical Park
Maps: USGS Hanapepe and Kekaha, though neither is really needed
Trail contact: Hawai'i Department of Land and Natural Resources; (808) 274-3444; www.hawaiistateparks.org
Special considerations: Go early or late in the day. It can be hot.

Finding the trailhead: From Lihue drive west on HI 50 (the Kaumuali'i Highway) almost to the town of Waimea. Just before

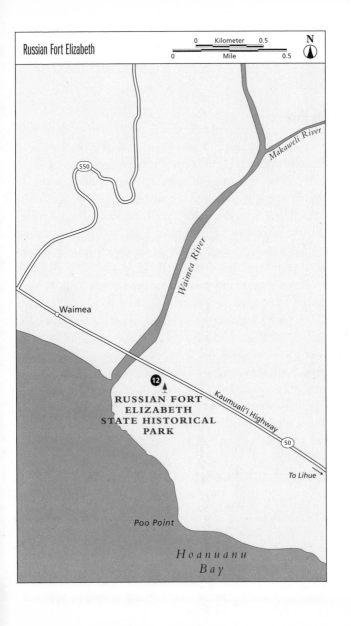

Russian Fort Elizabeth

Kilometer

Mile

N

550

Makaweli River

Waimea River

Waimea

12

**RUSSIAN FORT
ELIZABETH
STATE HISTORICAL
PARK**

Kaumuali'i Highway

50

To Lihue

Poo Point

*H o a n u a n u
B a y*

the mouth of the Waimea River you will see the turnoff for the fort marked on the *makai* (toward the sea) side of the road. There is a bathroom and water at the trailhead. **Trailhead GPS:** N21 57.08' / W159 39.47'

The Hike

Be sure to examine the interpretive panel at the trailhead beneath the broad umbrellas of monkeypod trees. A loose sort of loop starts to the right, heading counterclockwise around the fort, sometimes outside, sometimes within its walls. There are a few marker posts scattered here and there, but you have to have memorized the information on the trailhead panel to know what they mean. A little trail map would be useful, but is not available.

Begin outside the wall (notice how it was built without mortar.) The route then goes inside the fort, where you have to use your imagination to visualize what it may have been like. A set of steep stone steps takes you up onto the wall, where you can look out over the ocean beyond the *kiawe* trees. Return to the gap in the wall (near post 3). While the map on the board shows a trail continuing on around the fort, it is completely overgrown. You can instead follow a little path down to the beach and back. From a distance, you can see that the fort was built in a sort of star shape with lookout positions at each of the points.

Return as you came.

13 Koke'e State Park Nature Trail

This is a very short hike that you should take before setting out on any of the other trails around Koke'e State Park because it will help you identify some of the trees, ferns, and flowers you will see in the surrounding forests. Even more important, it will help you appreciate what a rare and valuable environment Kaua'i still supports. Several of the specimens described along the nature trail are found nowhere else in the world. You can pick up a free trail guide at the Koke'e Museum. Remember to return it when you're finished. (You can also buy your own to keep. The booklet itself is a handmade little work of art.)

Distance: 0.25-mile loop
Approximate hiking time: 30 minutes
Elevation gain: 50 feet
Trail surface: Grass and worn lava
Other trail users: None
Canine compatibility: Dogs on leash permitted
Fees and permits: None

Schedule: Open daily from 10:00 a.m. to 4:00 p.m.
Seasons: Year-round, though winter has more rain and mud
Land status: Koke'e State Park
Maps: *USGS Ha'ena,* but the trail guide from the Koke'e Museum is all you need
Trail contact: Koke'e Museum; (808) 335-9975; www.kokee.org

Finding the trailhead: From the Lihue Airport turn left (south) onto HI 51 (the Kapule Highway) to Rice Street. Turn right (northwest) and travel through town to HI 50 (the Kaumuali'i Highway). Turn left (southwest), and drive about 25 miles to Waimea. Turn right (north) on Waimea Canyon Drive (HI 550). It's not clearly marked, but if you miss it, never fear. Continue on to HI 552 (Koke'e Road) which is clearly marked with a big sign for Waimea Canyon and

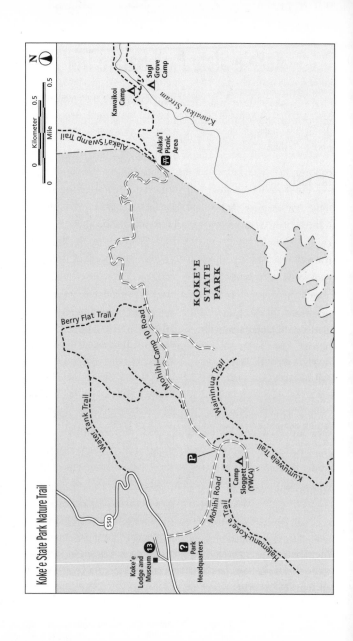

Koke'e State Park Nature Trail

N

0   Kilometer   0.5

0   Mile   0.5

Kawaikoi Camp

Sugi Grove Camp

Kawaikoi Stream

Alaka'i Swamp Trail

Alaka'i Picnic Area

KOKE'E STATE PARK

Berry Flat Trail

Mohihi-Camp 10 Road

Waininiua Trail

Water Tank Trail

Kumuwela Trail

550

P

Mohihi Road

Camp Sloggett (YWCA)

Halemanu-Koke'e Trail

Koke'e Lodge and Museum 13

Park Headquarters

Koke'e State Park. Turn right (*mauka*/toward the mountain). The two roads, 550 and 552, come together 7 miles later. Continue ascending the winding road for 8 miles more to Koke'e Lodge and Museum on the left, beyond a wide grassy picnic area. There are cabins for rent, a coffee shop (open only for breakfast and lunch), and a wonderful little museum, along with restrooms, cold drinks, and a telephone. **Trailhead GPS:** N22 07.52' / W159 39.32'

The Hike

The trail begins slightly behind and between the Koke'e Museum and the store where the famous Kaua'i chickens . . . er . . . jungle fowl cluck and squabble over chicken feed tourists can buy for them. There are thirty stops along the trail, each corresponding to a plant or tree, with information about its ecology, mythology, and use by native Hawaiians described in the guide. Some are wonderful for their names alone. *'Uki'uki* is a member of the lily family with bright blue berries. *Ohe ohe* is a striking tree with glossy leaves endemic to Hawai'i. *Koa,* a member of the pea family, is Hawaii's most important forest tree. Its extraordinary leaves deserve a close examination. Young trees have two different kinds of leaves on the same branch. When leaves first sprout from their buds they are small and pinnately divided, rather fernlike, but as they mature, the tiny leaves disappear and the petioles (the stems that attach the leaves to the twig) flatten and expand to a sickle shape that looks like a leaf itself. This might be an adaptation that helps the tree conserve moisture.

The trail ends at the edge of Kanaloahuluhulu Meadow. Before you return to the museum, glance across the meadow to the green forest on the far side. Most of the trees there are conifers introduced to Hawai'i from forests all over the world.

14 Pu'uka'ohelo–Berry Flat Trail

This is a cool and lovely, often misty, walk among a crazy mixture of tropical flowers, California redwoods, Japanese cedars, and other surprises. Many were planted as experimental forests in the 1930s by the Civilian Conservation Corps. Part of the route is along dirt (mud) road winding through the back lanes of down-home Hawaii. It is described beginning at Koke'e State Park Headquarters because not only is the road a beautiful walk in itself, it is not passable by ordinary passenger cars even when dry, and when wet is tricky even for four-wheel-drive vehicles.

Distance: 5.5-mile lollipop
Approximate hiking time: 2 to 3 hours
Elevation change: 400 feet
Trail surface: Some dirt road, some well-graded trail
Other trail users: A few four-wheel-drive vehicles and cyclists on the road portion of the hike
Seasons: Year-round. It rains more in winter, when there is more chance of slippery mud
Canine compatibility: Dogs are permitted on the road, though dogs in nearby residences might be territorial
Fees and permits: None
Schedule: Open daily from 10:00 a.m. to 4:00 p.m.

Land status: Koke'e State Park
Maps: *USGS Ha'ena; Northwestern Kaua'i Recreation Map* (Earthwalk Press)
Trail contact: Koke'e Museum; (808) 335-9975; www.kokee.org
Special considerations: Do not be tempted to take an ordinary passenger car down the Mohihi Road. Car rental agencies say you're on your own if you get stuck. Furthermore, it's slippery and dangerous when wet, and even in a four-wheel-drive vehicle you can slide off the road when mud fills in the tread on your tires. Walking is safer, easier, and more fun.

Please do not trespass on private property along the road.

Finding the trailhead: From the Lihue Airport turn left (south) on HI 51 (the Kapule Highway) to Rice Street. Turn right (northwest), traveling through town, to HI 50 (the Kaumuali'i Highway). Turn left (southwest), and drive about 25 miles to Waimea. Turn right (north) on Waimea Canyon Drive (HI 550). It's not clearly marked, but if you miss it continue to HI 552 (the Koke'e Road), which is clearly marked with a big sign for Waimea Canyon and Koke'e State Park. The two roads, HI 550 and HI 552, come together 7 miles later. Continue ascending the winding road 8 miles more to Koke'e Lodge and Museum on the left (north), beyond a wide grassy picnic area. There are cabins for rent, a coffee shop (open only for breakfast and lunch), and a great museum (not to mention restrooms, cold drinks, and a telephone.) **Trailhead GPS:** N22 07.45' / W159 39.31'

The Hike

Follow the driveway out of the Koke'e Museum area to HI 550 and turn left (east). Almost immediately turn right (south) onto an unmarked road with a sign marked YWCA CAMP SLOGGETT. This becomes the Mohihi Road, though you're not likely to see a street sign anywhere.

The stroll along the road is a delight for wildflower lovers, especially in spring and summer. There are fuchsias, elderberries, daisies, nasturtiums, ginger, hydrangeas, irises, orchids, and more. Unfortunately, all of these are nonnative intruders, some of which have overrun rare native Hawaiian species. The worst culprit is banana poka, a kind of passion flower introduced to Hawai'i from South America. Its flowers are some of the most intricate and beautiful in the world, and the fruits are delicious, if somewhat slimy in texture, and are used to flavor all kinds of pastries, snacks, and desserts in Hawai'i. Unfortunately, beautiful and delicious as they are, two species of passion flower have escaped

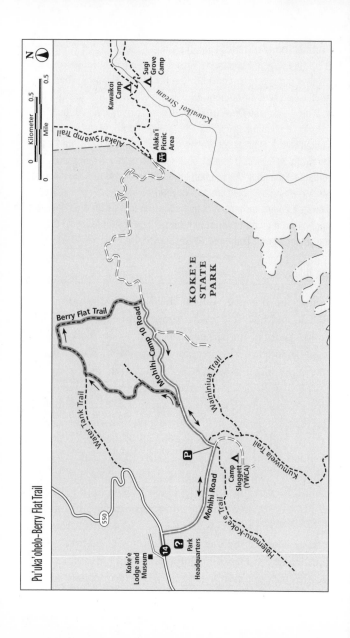

Pu'uka'ohelo-Berry Flat Trail

Koke'e Lodge and Museum

Park Headquarters

Water Tank Trail

Berry Flat Trail

Mohihi-Camp 10 Road

Mohihi Road

Camp Sloggett (YWCA)

Halemanu-Koke'e Trail

Kumuwela Trail

Waininiua Trail

KOKE'E STATE PARK

Alaka'i Picnic Area

Alaka'i Swamp Trail

Kawaikoi Camp

Sugi Grove Camp

Kawaikoi Stream

N

Kilometer   0   0.5

Mile   0   0.5

550

14

cultivation to become terrible pests. Feel free to pick and eat as many of the fruits as you like.

When you reach the turnoff to Camp Sloggett on your right (south), keep left (east) on the main road. Just beyond the junction is a sign marking a parking area (for four-wheel-drive vehicles) for the Halemanu-Koke'e, Kumu-wela, and Waininiua Trails. Immediately beyond the road splits again; keep left (north). Continue on the main road, ignoring other spurs heading off into the bushes. Most of these are private driveways. You'll pass two chain-link-encircled water treatment plants along the way.

Reach yet another unmarked Y junction. The two forks appear identical and will take you to one end or the other of the Berry Flat Trail. For now take the left fork, traveling the loop in a clockwise direction, and in about 0.25 mile reach a clearing with a sign marking the PU'UKA'OHELO TRAIL on the left (northwest). Leave the road and follow the path into the forest.

The narrow trail winds through dense strawberry guava bushes beneath a taller canopy of native *koa* trees. In 0.5 mile you'll reach a junction with the Water Tank Trail, which goes left (west) back toward the Koke'e Museum and Koke'e Road. This junction is not shown on older maps. Keep right (northeast) on the fork marked BERRY FLAT TRAIL and enter another world.

California redwoods filter the sunlight falling on bright green ferns and mosses. Japanese sugi cypresses and occasional ginger plants are all that remind you you're not in California. At what appears to be another three-way junction keep right (southeast) on the Berry Flat Trail. The unmarked third fork goes nowhere at all.

Eventually the redwoods begin to thin out a little and

you find yourself among the berry bushes that give the trail its name. In just a small patch are crammed almost every kind of berry imaginable: raspberries, blackberries, elderberries, and even strawberries. The trail abruptly ends at the Mohihi Road, which you follow to the right (west). Keep right (west) at a second junction and in another 0.25 mile find yourself back where the two forks of the loop converge. Go straight ahead, back to the PARK HERE sign and trailhead, turn right (west), and continue on back to HI 550 and Koke'e headquarters.

Miles and Directions

0.0   Start at the Koke'e headquarters turnoff. Turn left (east) onto HI 550

0.2   Turn right (south) on the road marked YWCA CAMP SLOGGETT (N22 07.46' / W159 39.25')

1.3   Camp Sloggett turnoff. Keep left (west) to the PARK HERE sign, then immediately turn left (north).

1.8   Unmarked Y junction; take the left (north-northeast) fork (N22 07.40' / W159 38.50')

2.1   Pu'uka'ohelo Trail; turn left

2.2   Berry Flat-Water Tank trail junction; keep right (north) on Berry Flat Trail (N22 08.06' / W159 38.40')

3.2   Berry Flat/Mohihi Road junction; turn right (west) onto road and right (west) again at first junction (N22 07.51' / W159 38.21)

3.7   Return to unmarked Y junction; go straight ahead

5.5   Return the way you came to HI 550 and Koke'e State Park headquarters

15 Cliff Trail

Enjoy exhilarating views into and across Waimea Canyon, the Grand Canyon of the Pacific, in a setting of tropical vegetation and solitude instead of among other tourists beside a parking lot. There are a few ups and downs on this pleasant walk, but since most of it is on country road, none of it is steep. There are lots of wildflowers, including ginger and orchids, as well as many native Hawaiian species to admire along the way. The trailhead is convenient to the headquarters of Koke'e State Park and is the starting point for many other destinations if you're looking for a longer outing.

Distance: 1.8 miles out and back
Approximate hiking time: 1 to 2 hours
Elevation change: 800 feet
Trail surface: Mostly dirt road
Other trail users: Occasional four-wheel-drive vehicles
Canine compatibility: Dogs on leash permitted

Fees and permits: None
Schedule: Open daily from 10:00 a.m. to 4:00 p.m.
Land status: Koke'e State Park
Maps: *USGS Ha'ena; Northwestern Kaua'i Recreation Map* (Earthwalk Press)
Trail contact: Koke'e Museum; (808) 335-9975; www.kokee.org

Finding the trailhead: From the Lihue Airport turn left (south) on HI 51 (the Kapule Highway) to Rice Street. Turn right (northwest), traveling through town, to HI 50 (the Kaumuali'i Highway). Turn left (southwest), and drive about 25 miles to Waimea. Turn right (north) on Waimea Canyon Drive (HI 550). It's not clearly marked, but if you miss it continue to HI 552 (the Koke'e Road), marked with a sign for Waimea Canyon and Koke'e State Park. The two roads, HI 550 and HI 552, come together 7 miles later. Continue ascending for 8 miles to Koke'e Lodge and Museum on the left (north).

From the museum/lodge area at Koke'e State Park, drive south for about 1 mile down HI 550 to about milepost 14 and signs marking the boundary of Koke'e State Park. Park on the right (east) side of the road. The trail begins across the street at Halemanu Road (restricted to four-wheel-drive vehicles). **Trailhead GPS:** N22 06.57' / W159 40.10'

The Hike

Follow Halemanu Road, lined with ginger, fairly steeply downhill for about 0.5 mile to where the grade levels out. Just as the road begins to rise again, reach a junction with the signed Canyon/Cliff Trail at mile 0.7, where you turn right (south) to follow the trail.

Very soon you will arrive at a wide and usually muddy spot in the road where there may be some four-wheel-drive vehicles parked. A sign reading CANYON TRAIL 2.9 MILES directs you straight ahead (south). Follow the trail for just a few more yards before continuing on the signed Cliff Trail, which angles off to the right (south). (The sign says CLIFF VIEW POINT.) In only another 0.1 mile reach a green pipe fence marking the edge of a cliff. The trail follows the fence as it bends left for a few more yards to a breathtaking view down magnificent Waimea Canyon. White tropic birds soar along the red cliffs and the winding river sparkles at the bottom, lined with a silvery canopy of *kukuis,* Hawaii's state tree.

Off to the left (east) look for a length of bare red dirt amid the greenery that is a section of the Canyon Trail leading to the top of Waipo'o Falls. You can't see the waterfall from here, but occasionally its presence is revealed when a gust of wind sends up a puff of spray. Just beyond this and

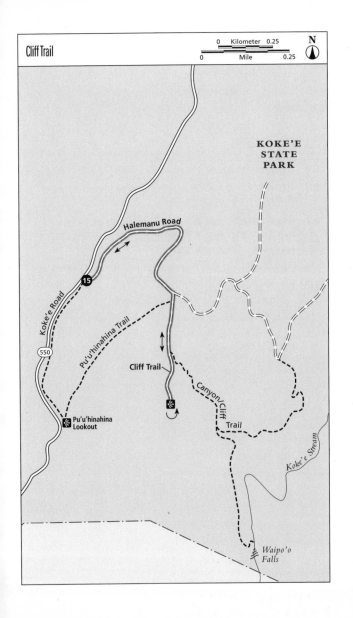

Cliff Trail

0   Kilometer   0.25
0   Mile   0.25

N

KOKE'E
STATE
PARK

Halemanu Road

Koke'e Road

550

15

Pu'u'hinahina Trail

Cliff Trail

Pu'u'hinahina
Lookout

Canyon Cliff

Trail

Koke'e Stream

Waipo'o
Falls

a bit to its left, look for an unusually big window, a hole in the lava cliff.

Do not try to go beyond the sign that marks the end of the trail. It's extremely steep, slippery, and a long, long way down.

Miles and Directions

0.0 Trailhead at beginning of road (N22 06.57' / W159 40.10')

0.6 Turn right (south) at the sign that says CANYON AND CLIFF TRAILS. (N22 06.55' / W159 39.55')

0.7 Reach the wide spot in the road with a sign that says Canyon Trail is straight ahead. In just a few yards turn right (south) at CLIFF VIEW POINT sign.

0.9 Viewpoint and end of Cliff Trail (N22 06.38' / W159 54.82')

1.8 Return to trailhead

16 Pu'u'hinahina Lookout Loop

This is at the upper end of "easy" because it is pretty steep down and up, but the trail isn't very long. You can make a detour of only a few minutes to look over the Cliff Trail viewpoint first, then pass the ridge that blocks your view to the south in order to get a look at Waipo'o Falls, invisible from the Cliff Trail, from the Pu'u'hinahina Lookout. You have to share the view with lots of people who have "hiked" only a few feet from a nearby parking lot, but you have the satisfaction of the journey as well as a bonus: an excellent view of forbidden Ni'ihau Island.

Distance: 2.4-mile loop
Approximate hiking time: 2 to 3 hours
Elevation gain: 800 feet
Trail surface: Part dirt road, part weathered lava, some concrete path, some highway verge
Other trail users: None on the trail; watch for cars and bicycles on the highway

Canine compatibility: Dogs permitted on leash
Fees and permits: None
Schedule: Open daily from 10:00 a.m. to 4:00 p.m.
Land status: Koke'e State Park
Maps: USGS Ha'ena; Northwestern Kaua'i Recreation Map (Earthwalk Press)
Trail contact: Koke'e Museum; (808) 335-9975; www.kokee.org

Finding the trailhead: From the Lihue Airport turn left (south) on HI 51 (the Kapule Highway) to Rice Street. Turn right (northwest), traveling through town, to HI 50 (the Kaumuali'i Highway). Turn left (southwest), and drive about 25 miles to Waimea. Turn right (north) on Waimea Canyon Drive (HI 550). It's not clearly marked; if you miss it continue to HI 552 (the Koke'e Road), marked with a sign for Waimea Canyon and Koke'e State Park. The two roads, HI 550 and HI 552, come together 7 miles beyond. Continue ascending for 8 miles to Koke'e Lodge and Museum on the left (north). From the museum/lodge area at Koke'e State Park, drive south for about 1 mile on HI 550 to about milepost 14 and signs marking the boundary of Koke'e State Park. Park on the right (east) side of the road. The trail begins across the street at the Halemanu Road (restricted to four-wheel-drive vehicles). **Trailhead GPS:** N22 06.57' / W159 40.10'

The Hike

Follow the Halemanu Road fairly steeply downhill for about 0.5 mile to where the grade levels out. Just as the road begins to rise again, reach a junction with the signed Canyon/Cliff Trail at mile 0.7, and you turn right (south). Arrive at a wide usually muddy spot in the road where some four-wheel-drive vehicles may be parked. A sign here says CANYON TRAIL 2.9 MILES. *In back* of this sign, *facing the other direction (southward)*, is another sign for Pu'u'hinahina Lookout. As you face this smaller sign, turn left (west) along a narrow, less conspicuous path, leaving the dirt road.

Descend steeply on switchbacks (careful, it's slippery), among Hawaiian native plants like *maile*, the vine used for wedding leis, down into a narrow gully lined with huge impatiens and fuchsias. Hop the gulch and scramble steeply back up the other side toward a big *koa* tree. A series of steep switchbacks climbs up the drier, firmer side of the gully among small *ohia* trees and *pukiawe* berry bushes.

At about the same time the trail begins to level out, you will probably be able to hear highway traffic, and shortly thereafter arrive at the busy parking area. Continue straight ahead along the paved path to the overlook. Soak up the panorama and look for the lower end of Waipo'o Falls off

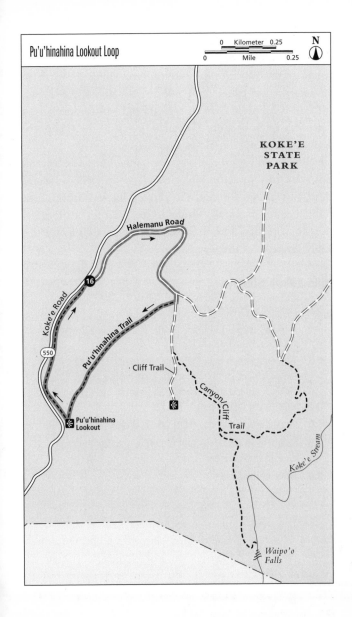

Pu'u'hinahina Lookout Loop

0   Kilometer   0.25
0   Mile   0.25

N

KOKE'E
STATE
PARK

Halemanu Road

16

Koke'e Road

550

Pu'u'hinahina Trail

Cliff Trail

Canyon/Cliff Trail

Pu'u'hinahina
Lookout

Koke'e Stream

Waipo'o
Falls

to the left (southeast). To get to the Ni'ihau overlook, walk down a few stair steps to the parking lot, turn left before reaching the bathrooms, and continue along the path to an interpretive panel with information about the island. Ni'ihau is privately owned, *kapu* (forbidden) to outsiders, a place inhabited by pure Hawaiians living in the traditional way and speaking the Hawaiian language.

You could return the way you came, but probably will not want to repeat the long down-and-up route a second time. Instead, go through the parking lot to HI 550, turn right (north), and walk alongside the road for a short 0.5 mile to your car. The shoulder is wide enough to do this safely for most of the way back.

Miles and Directions

0.0   Halemanu Road trailhead

0.6   Turn right (south) at the Canyon/Cliff Trail junction (N22 06.55' / W159 39.55')

0.7   Turn right (west) onto the clear but small trail leading from the wide spot in the road at the CANYON TRAIL 2.9 MILES sign. *Or* walk around to the back of this sign to the sign pointing west to the Pu'u'hinahina Trail.

1.5   Pu'u'hinahina overlook (N22 06.34' / W159 40.11')

2.0   Return to HI 550, turn right (north), and follow the verge back toward your car

2.4   Arrive at trailhead

17 Kaluapuhi Trail

This easy, flat walk takes you where the air is cool, the foliage lush, and the birds plentiful. It doesn't go anywhere in particular, simply from one spot on the road through Koke'e State Park to another, but in the past its main attraction was a grove of introduced Methley plum trees whose small, tart fruits were eagerly harvested in summer. The trees are still there, but have not been producing much in recent years, so don't be disappointed if you don't find any. (You can probably find some strawberries and blackberries instead.) If you prefer your hike to end with a little more excitement, you can add a 0.5-mile walk to the spectacular Kalalau Lookout.

Distance: 2.4 miles out and back; 1.2-mile shuttle
Approximate hiking time: 1 hour
Elevation change: Rolling terrain; maybe 100 feet
Trail surface: Mostly grass
Other trail users: None
Canine compatibility: Dogs permitted

Fees and permits: None
Schedule: Open daily from 10:00 a.m. to 4:00 p.m.
Land status: Koke'e State Park
Maps: *USGS Ha'ena; Northwestern Kaua'i Recreation Map* (Earthwalk Press)
Trail contact: Koke'e Museum; (808) 335-9975; www.kokee.org

Finding the trailhead: From the Lihue Airport turn left (south) on HI 51 (the Kapule Highway) to Rice Street. Turn right (northwest), traveling through town to HI 50 (the Kaumuali'i Highway). Turn left (southwest) and drive about 25 miles to Waimea. Turn right (north) on Waimea Canyon Drive (HI 550). It's not clearly marked so if you miss it continue to HI 552 (the Koke'e Road), marked with a big sign for Waimea Canyon and Koke'e State Park. The two roads, HI 550

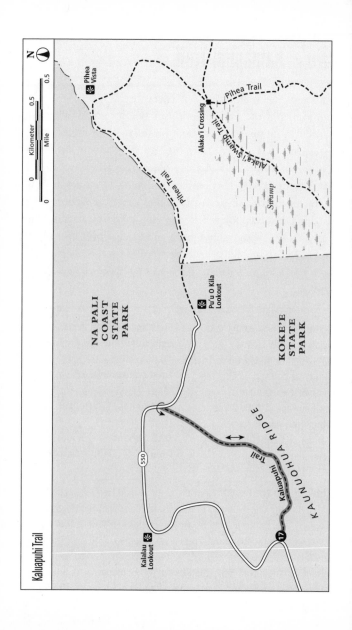

Kaluapuhi Trail

N

Kilometer 0.5
Mile 0.5

Pihea Vista

Pihea Trail

Alaka'i Crossing

Alaka'i Swamp Trail

Swamp

Pihea Trail

Pu'u O Kila Lookout

NA PALI COAST STATE PARK

KOKE'E STATE PARK

550

Kalalau Lookout

Kaluapuhi Trail

KAUNUOHUA RIDGE

17

and HI 552, come together 7 miles beyond. Continue ascending the winding road, passing Koke'e Lodge on your left (north), to a point just beyond milepost 17 and the Awa'awapuhi Trailhead, which is on the left (northwest). The signed Kaluapuhi Trailhead is on the right (east). Park along the side of the road. **Trailhead GPS:** N22 08.32' / W159 38.46'

The Hike

Head uphill at the trail sign for a very few minutes until the trail begins its gentle rolling up-and-down course. The vegetation on either side is high and thick with red powder-puff *ohia lehua* trees and mountain *naupaka* bushes, which have white flowers with purple stripes along each petal, and each blossom looks as though it has been torn in half. According to legend, the flowers of the *naupaka* were ripped apart by a beautiful maiden who challenged her lover to find and bring her the other half. The "other half" may be growing along the island's shore where a different species, beach *naupaka,* has similar one-sided flowers.

Plenty of nonnative species grow here as well, including *uluhe* (false staghorn) fern, banana poka, and of course, Methley plum trees. The greatest concentration of these is about halfway along the trail on the right (east). Watch for an obscure opening in the bushes made by other hikers. Here and there you'll see muddy gouges in the earth where pigs have been rooting in the soil. If you arrive early in the morning or late in the afternoon you'll probably see pheasants and other ground birds foraging in the grass.

When you get to trail's end you will find yourself at a signed, but otherwise obscure, spot on the highway. Retrace your steps to the trailhead. If you have arranged a shuttle or a ride, this is the end of your hike.

Miles and Directions

0.0 Lower trailhead

1.2 Upper trailhead and turnaround point; end of the trail if done as a shuttle (N22 08.58/W159 38.15)

2.4 Return to trailhead (if out and back)

Options: From the northern end of the Kaluapuhi Trail you can turn left and walk west for about 0.5 mile along HI 550 to the Kalalau Lookout for a breathtaking view (weather permitting) of the Na Pali Coast. There are bathrooms but no water at the lookout. Alternatively, you can turn right (east) and follow the road for about 0.5 mile to its end at the Pihea Trailhead and lookout.

18 Upper Pihea Trail

This hike follows the first part of the most direct route into the Alaka'i Swamp. It is also the only place anywhere near a road that directly overlooks the swamp, but you will be lucky if the clouds part long enough for you to see into it. That's not all there is to see, however. On the northwest side of the path you'll find several opportunities to experience heart-stopping views 4,000 feet straight down onto what might be the world's most beautiful coastline at Kalalau Beach, and the clouds are less likely to interfere.

Distance: 2 miles out and back
Approximate hiking time: 1 to 2 hours
Elevation change: 100 feet
Trail surface: Mostly abandoned red clay road; slippery when wet
Other trail users: None
Canine compatibility: Dogs permitted on leash
Fees and permits: None
Schedule: Open daily from 10:00 a.m. to 4:00 p.m.

Land status: Koke'e State Park
Maps: USGS Ha'ena; Northwestern Kaua'i Recreation Map (Earthwalk Press)
Trail contact: Koke'e Museum; (808) 335-9975; www.kokee.org
Special considerations: The trail is usually quite broad, but is sometimes lined with dense vegetation and the visibility may be poor. Keep a close watch on small children.

Finding the trailhead: From the Lihue Airport turn left (south) on HI 51 (the Kapule HI) to Rice Street. Turn right (northwest) through town to HI 50 (the Kaumuali'i Highway), turn left (southwest), and drive about 25 miles to Waimea. Turn right (north) on Waimea Canyon Drive (HI 550). It's not clearly marked; if you miss it continue to HI 552 (the Koke'e Road), which is marked with a big sign for Waimea Canyon and Koke'e State Park. The two roads, HI 550 and HI 552, come together 7 miles later. Continue ascending, passing

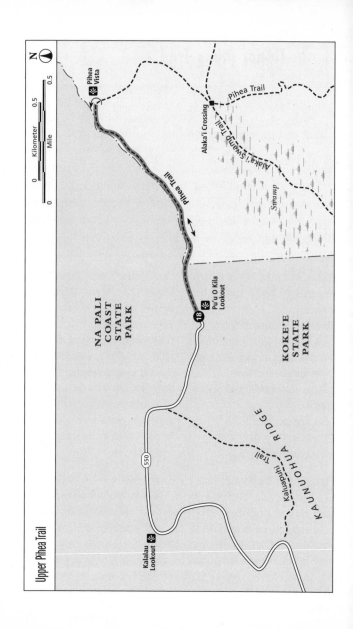

Upper Pihea Trail

Koke'e State Park headquarters, beyond which the road becomes more narrow, winding, potholed, and patched. Pass Kalalau Lookout (your last chance for a bathroom) at mile 18, where the road becomes miraculously smooth and perfect again. The highway ends less than 1 mile beyond the lookout at the Pihea Trailhead and Pu'u O Kila lookout. There is a large parking lot but no facilities. **Trailhead GPS:** N22 08.51' / W159 37.52'

The Hike

Wind up the asphalt path to the trailhead sign that says PIHEA VISTA. The view from the lookout is spectacular even if you don't go any farther, with the Kalalau Valley *makai* (toward the ocean), and the Alaka'i Swamp *mauka* (toward the mountain). A sign points toward Mount Wai'ale'ale, said to be the wettest place on earth, but chances are the sign is all you will ever see of the mountain behind the clouds. The mist that swirls around the Kalalau Valley and the Na Pali Coast to the northwest is not nearly so dense, and if you are willing to wait a few minutes, there is a good chance it will blow away long enough to reveal a bit of Kalalau Beach and the unbelievably blue sea at the base of the almost vertical black cliff.

Just beyond the lookout the pavement ends at a sign marking the beginning of the trail, and you begin a descent along a broad bare ridgetop, all that remains of a misguided attempt to build a road connecting Koke'e State Park with the road at Ha'ena State Park, making a highway all the way around the island. The road was originally planned to follow the ridge ahead of you down into and across part of the swamp, but you will only have to walk along this route for a few minutes to understand why that plan had to be abandoned.

The trail flattens out and becomes narrower, muddier, more rutted, and overgrown as you progress. Where the road finally peters out, a short spur heads uphill to the left (northwest) to Pihea Vista for another view into the Kalalau Valley. It's a muddy scramble involving loose handholds and precarious balancing on slimy tree roots, but it gives you a little broader view of the coast.

This is your turnaround point. The Pihea Trail makes a sharp right and drops steeply down into the Alaka'i Swamp from the vista; beyond this point, you leave the "easy" category. If you decide to sample just a bit of the swamp, please remember that it is going to be a stiff, hot climb back up and there is no water.

Miles and Directions

0.0 Pu'u O Kila lookout
1.0 Pihea Vista (N22 09.15' / W159 37.33')
2.0 Return to trailhead

19 Iliau Nature Trail

The trail through this Alice in Wonderland grove, part of Waimea Canyon State Park, has recently been given a thorough renovation with shiny new signs identifying the plants along the route and adding fascinating bits of lore about each. You don't need signs to tell you that the things growing around you are no ordinary roses and petunias, but weird and rare organisms utterly unlike anything you have ever seen. The stars of the show are the pompons-on-sticks—the *iliau*—that grow only here on Kaua'i. This is also good place to enjoy breathtaking views down into Waimea Canyon without cars whizzing along a highway just behind you.

Distance: 0.4-mile loop
Approximate hiking time: 20 to 30 minutes
Elevation change: Very little
Trail surface: Fairly smooth lava
Other trail users: None
Canine compatibility: Dogs not permitted

Fees and permits: None
Schedule: Open daily from 10:00 a.m. to 4:00 p.m.
Land status: Waimea Canyon State Park
Maps: USGS *Waimea Canyon*, though none is needed
Trail contact: Koke'e Museum; (808) 335-9975; www.kokee.org

Finding the trailhead: From the Lihue Airport turn left (south) on HI 51 (the Kapule Highway) to Rice Street. Turn right (northwest) through town to HI 50 (the Kaumuali'i Highway). Turn left (southwest) and drive about 25 miles to Waimea. Turn right (north) on Waimea Canyon Drive (HI 550). It's not clearly marked; if you miss it continue to HI 552 (the Koke'e Road), which is marked with a sign for Waimea Canyon and Koke'e State Park. The two roads, HI 550 and HI 552 come together 7 miles later. The trailhead is between mileposts 8 and 9, on HI 550, on the right (east) side of the road. There is a not-very-obvious brown and gold trail sign right next to an emergency call box. Park along the east side of the road (opposite the trailhead) and lock your car. There are no facilities. **Trailhead GPS:** N27 05.26' / W159 66.09'

The Hike

Climb up the bank to a bench beneath a shady tree. Turn to the right (east) and descend a few steps to find yourself in a grove of, among other things, upside-down mops or pompons on sticks, some with big bouquets of little flowers erupting from their tops in spring and summer. These are the iliau (*Wilkesia* sp.), whose ancestor was a small member of the sunflower family that was transported, most likely by a bird, 2,500 miles over the sea from the Americas. In Hawai'i it evolved into oddities like the silversword that grows in the barren red cinders on Haleakala on Maui, the greensword of the Maui bogs, and the iliau. It retains its pompon-on-a-stick form for two to ten years, after which it shoots up a 4-foot stalk right out of the center of the leaves, along which are slender, drooping stems tipped with yellowish puffball flowers. Then it dies.

At about 0.2 mile, you come to a signed junction with the Kukui Trail, which heads straight ahead down into Waimea Canyon. The nature trail keeps left (north) here and describes a more or less oval path (traveling counterclockwise), part of which runs near the edge of the cliff where the views out over Waimea Canyon are the best.

Among the other inhabitants of this garden is the *a'ali'i,* a shrub with clustered, reddish, winged fruits. These are hops, related to the ones used to make beer. Another is *pukiawe,* with small short leaves reminiscent of a conifer. It

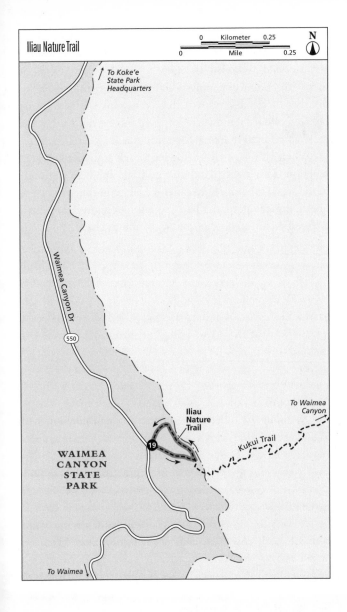

Iliau Nature Trail

To Koke'e
State Park
Headquarters

Waimea Canyon Dr

550

Iliau
Nature
Trail

Kukui Trail

To Waimea
Canyon

WAIMEA
CANYON
STATE
PARK

19

To Waimea

N

has lots of very small pink and white berries, a favorite of *nenes* (Hawaiian geese), which were used by the Hawaiian *ali'i,* or chiefs, who had so much power that they could not mix with common people without polluting themselves or injuring their subjects. A bath in the smoke from burning pukiawe would temporarily dissolve this barrier so that the chief could behave like a normal human now and then.

When you have closed the loop back at the Kukui Trail junction, turn right (west) and go back uphill to the trailhead. If you are not ready to return yet, you can walk a few hundred yards along the Kukui Trail to a grassy area with a covered picnic table, then return to the trailhead.

About the Author

Suzanne Swedo, director of W.I.L.D. (natural history adventures around the world), has backpacked the mountains of every continent. She has led groups into the wilderness for over twenty-five years and teaches wilderness survival and natural sciences to individuals, schools, universities, museums, and organizations such as Yosemite Association and the Sierra Club. She is author of *Best Easy Day Hikes Yosemite National Park, Hiking Yosemite, Hiking California's Golden Trout Wilderness,* and *Adventure Travel Tips,* all FalconGuides. She lectures and consults about backpacking, botany, and survival on radio and television, as well as in print.